The Practical Workshop

A Woodworker's Guide to Workbenches, Layout & Tools

W9-ARB-833

DISCARD
Valparaiso - Porter Cou~
Library Syst~~

Porter County Public Library

Kouts Public Library
101 E. Daumer Road
Kouts, IN 46347

kabnf   KO
684.08 SCHWA

Schwarz, Christopher, 1968- author
The practical workshop
33410014422358   06/13/17

POPULAR
WOODWORKING
BOOKS
CINCINNATI, OHIO
popularwoodworking.com

By Christopher Schwarz
& the Editors of *Popular Woodworking*

Contents

The Practical Workshop

A Woodworker's Guide to Workbenches, Layout & Tools

Introduction

As the editor of a woodworking magazine, I got to see some of the most incredible (and humble) workshops all over the planet. Human nature being what it is, it's easiest to remember the workshops that were nicer than my house. I've visited several shops where the woodworker had a couple thousand square feet of organized space, wood storage that was accessed by a remote crane and a library room dedicated solely to reading books and watching woodworking videos. I don't begrudge the woodworkers who build their dream shops. Every one of them earned their shops with hard work, determination and inspiration. But I am here to tell you that the quality of the furniture that comes out of a shop is entirely independent of the physical space in which it was created. All the proof you need is to learn a little bit about Rob Millard, a professional Ohio furniture maker who specializes in Federal-era pieces (look him up on the internet), and works in a basement space that doesn't even really look like a shop. Most of his tools and machines are portable home-center stuff. His bench is unremarkable. And the white cinder-block walls look more like a prison than a space to build pieces that make your heart soar. But that's exactly what he does. If you are looking for a book that will help you build the ultimate dream shop, this is not the book you are looking for. If you are looking for the shortest and most effective way to set up shop so you can get to the good part – making furniture – then read on.

A Tradition of Practicality

For the last 20 years, *Popular Woodworking Magazine* has focused on offering workshop projects that are grounded in the "get-it-done" tradition you would find in professional workshops from the 18th century to the present day.

Yes, you need a good bench because it will make your life easier. But you don't need a French polished beauty that represents a tour de force of your woodworking skills. That fancy bench won't work any better than the basic benches used in production shops during the last 300 years. And so in this book we present two bench designs that can be built quickly using common framing lumber. These aren't slap-together designs you'll outgrow. They are based on hundreds of years of careful refinement by people who ate or starved based on their productivity. We also present the basic "appliances" that will make your work at your bench a bit easier. Again, these aren't for jig lovers – they are simple devices that have proven themselves for hundreds of years. That same practical philosophy applies to this book's section on setting up your machinery. Most woodworking shops have a few machines, and

there are long-standing rules for how work should flow through the shop. And so placing your machines is one of the most important tasks for the woodworker. Likewise, there are a few accessories you can build that will make your machines more suitable for making furniture (as opposed to building houses). A portable, stow-away router table, a stand for your miter saw and an outfeed table for your table saw are all helpful items for every shop. These designs also have the benefit of folding flat when not in use – so you can do more work in a smaller space. Finally, there's storage. You need it. If you don't get a handle on your lumber, your hand tools and even your nails and screws, then you will spend most of your shop time looking for your sandpaper, that bit of maple you stashed away or your No. 8 screws. And so a good portion of this book is focused on helping you rein in all the bits and pieces required for building furniture. But again, these projects are based on practicality. Make a lumber rack from a few sticks of framing lumber and pipe. Build a rolling tool box from a couple sheets of cabinet-grade plywood. Nail together a hanging cabinet that will store all your screws, nails and bits of hardware.

Aside from these projects, we also threw in a couple of fancy (but still practical) tool chests for your hand tools. Lest you think we are slipping, these sorts of chests are based on hundreds of years of professional work. In a traditional workshop, the tool chest or tool cabinet was the one place in the shop that was reserved to demonstrate the skill of the maker. And so you would see some fancy woods or a bit of marquetry that said: "Hey, I know what I'm doing." Yes, this works. My own basement shop is based on the principles outlined in this book – heck some of the projects in this book are in use in my shop today. My shop is a pretty small space – 15' x 20' and I share it with the furnace and a lot of ducts and pipes. And yet I am able to turn out large pieces of work, such as a 10' run of cabinets, with ease because my machines are arranged in a proper work triangle, my lumber is stored flat on the wall and all my tools and fasteners are within reach and well-organized. Do I wish my shop were nicer and bigger? Perhaps. It's difficult not to become envious of the dream shops we see in magazines and books. But does my shop have to be bigger or nicer to turn out chairs, cabinets, tables and beds? Nope. My shop works. And yours can, too, with the help of the projects and ideas in this book.

Christopher Schwarz
Fort Mitchell, Ky.
January 2017

Your First Toolkit

by Frank Klausz

When I came to America, I had a lovely wife, two suitcases and 50 bucks. Oh man, where do I start? Everybody needs a basic tool kit, especially if you want to do woodworking. I had a limited budget. Starting out in America, I got paid low wages even though I was a Master; they tried to blame it on my language skills. Thank God my first boss did not treat me well or I'd probably still be working for him!

I started to buy tools and build this toolbox. The first tool I got was a 10" dovetail saw. You need a marking gauge; I made one. I also bought a 6' folding ruler.

A week later I went to the same store and bought a nice set of chisels that included ⅛", ¼", ⅜", ½", ¾" and a 1" chisel. I bought a two-sided Arkansas oilstone, one side rough and the other super fine. The salesman wanted to sell me sharpening oil; I told him I use kerosene.

I kept going: A No. 4 Stanley smoothing plane, low-angle block plane, small hand saw, two hammers and two mallets — I made one on a lathe and the other is square. At a flea market I found an old Stanley No. 7 jointer plane.

I kept asking around about where to find old tools. I went to tool-collector meetings and tool sales. I found beautiful Stanley planes with Brazilian rosewood handles and brass fittings, and I began collecting them very fast.

But let's get back to the basic toolkit. To work wood, you need squares: a framing square and a couple of any brand of small squares, 8" or 6". Plus a 1" putty knife — make sure the blade is flexible — an awl and screwdrivers. You need at least five flat-head screwdrivers (your screwdriver should fit the screw) and three Phillips-head screwdrivers. Rasps: a Nicholson No. 50 patternmaker's rasp and bastard-cut rasp, a mill file, a cabinetmaker's scraper, a scraper burnisher, nail sets and pliers.

You need sanding blocks: one cork-bottom block for sanding wood and one felt block for sanding finish.

As you grow in your woodworking, your toolkit will grow with you. If you want to do veneering, you need a veneer saw, tape dispenser and a small roller. If you run into curves you need a compass plane and a spokeshave. I could go on and on.

Woodworking tools have come a long way. We have beautiful high-quality tools such as those by Lie-Nielsen Toolworks and Veritas/Lee Valley. And — finally — some of these quality tools come ready to use. My first dovetail saw needed serious work to make it work for me. I had to sharpen it and make the set smaller. Lie-Nielsen and Adria dovetail saws come sharpened and ready to go.

To enjoy woodworking, you need to have sharp tools. Invest in some good sharpening stones with at least two or three different grits. When buying chisels choose your brand carefully. I have tested about 10 different brands of chisels and found Marples the best bang for your buck. The company recently changed its name to Irwin Blue Chip Chisels.

Because the top of the handle of this brand is rounded and too smooth, I recommend making it flat on the top. Take off about ½"; you can sand it off with a disc sander or simply rasp it off.

Although you need basic tools to work wood, the most important tool in a workshop, especially for handwork, is a sturdy workbench like mine. It holds the wood for any task. With a bench like that, you will enjoy your work.

A Basic Toolbox

Your toolbox does not need to be large or fancy. This small one has served me well for 20 years, both by my workbench and out on jobs.

Try not to make your toolbox any larger than you have to. This toolbox was fine for the first 20 years, but if I made it again I would try to make it a little smaller. Whatever you do, make the toolbox fit your kit of tools.

Some construction details: The sides, front and back of my toolbox are made of Eastern white pine that I dovetailed together. Your toolbox does not need to be dovetailed. Finger joints are no problem. Miters would work. There are lots of ways to build a box.

The top and bottom of my toolbox are ½"-thick plywood pieces that are simply glued to the top and bottom of the box with a few finishing nails, too. You could put the top and bottom in a rabbet or a groove if you want to make it more complex.

The ½" horizontal plywood divider between the drawers and the open section of my toolbox rests in a groove in the box and the tool holders are attached to the side and back. This could be simplified. You could put glue blocks in the box and glue the divider to the glue blocks. What's important about the divider is that it not go all the way to the sides and back of the toolbox. The longer tools, such as the chisels and screwdrivers, drop all the way to the bottom of the toolbox. This is also why the drawers aren't the full depth of the box.

My drawers are dovetailed front and back. Yours don't have to be. To save space, I did not put the ¼"-plywood bottoms into a groove in the drawers. Instead, I cut a rabbet in the bottom of the drawer and put the bottom in that.

My toolbox sits on four feet nailed to the case. This makes the toolbox sit flat on irregular surfaces. You could use furniture glides instead or omit the feet.

It's your toolbox so it's your choice.

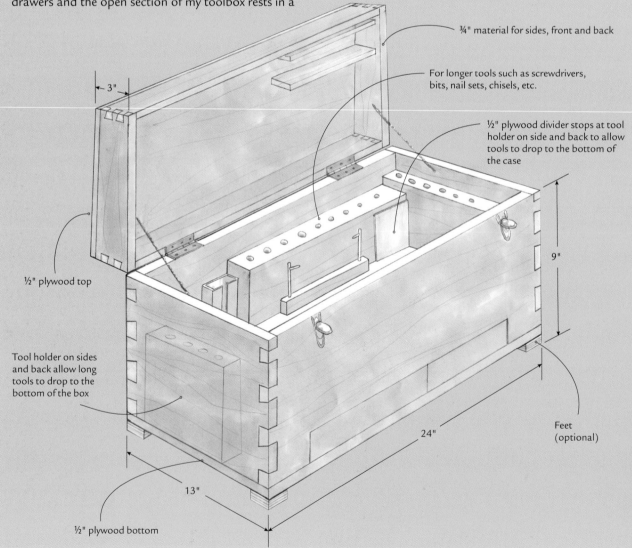

¾" material for sides, front and back

For longer tools such as screwdrivers, bits, nail sets, chisels, etc.

½" plywood divider stops at tool holder on side and back to allow tools to drop to the bottom of the case

½" plywood top

Tool holder on sides and back allow long tools to drop to the bottom of the box

9"

3"

24"

13"

Feet (optional)

½" plywood bottom

Illustration by Hayes Shanesy

The Basic Kit of Tools

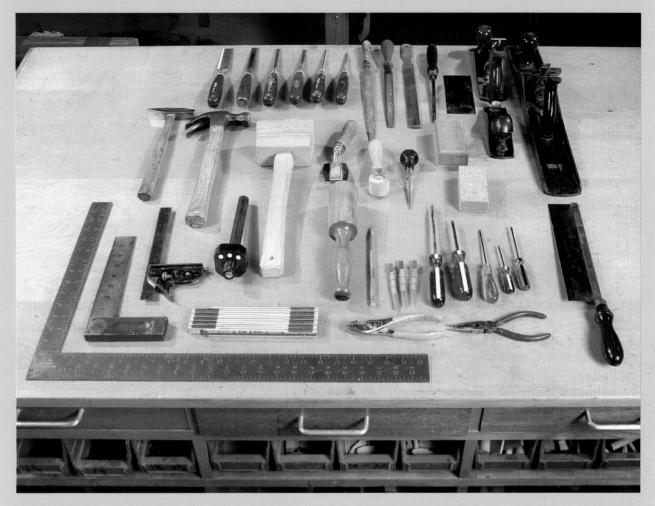

Below is a list of tools essential for good woodworking. These tools are widely available from a variety of sources, from your local home center, specialty stores and catalogs.

• Six bevel-edge chisels, ⅛", ¼", ⅜", ½", ¾" and 1". Two-sided oilstone (not shown).

• Nicholson No. 50 patternmaker's rasp, Nicholson half-round bastard-cut rasp, mill file.

• Burnisher and card scraper.

• No. 4-sized smoothing plane (9"-long sole), No. 7-sized jointer plane (22"-long sole), low-angle block plane.

• 16 oz. claw hammer, tack hammer, nail sets.

• Carpenter's mallet (16 oz.) for mortising, smaller-lathe turned mallet for chopping dovetails and other light work.

• Veneer saw, small edge roller.

• Scratch awl.

• Cork-faced sanding block, felt block.

• Screwdrivers. #0, #1 and #2 Phillips screwdrivers plus at least five straight (flat-head) screwdrivers.

• 10" dovetail saw. I like a rip saw filed with 15 to 16 TPI Either a straight or pistol-grip saw is fine. And if you prefer Japanese dovetail saws, that's fine, too.

• Steel framing square, 8" try square, 12" combination square, 6' folding extension rule. Tape measure (not shown).

• Marking gauge.

• Pliers, needle-nose pliers.

Butterfly Sawhorse

by Don Williams

Whether I'm working in the shop, remodeling or performing routine maintenance around the house, I am in constant need of a sturdy, lightweight worktable. The most popular one for, oh, the past 2,000 years, has been a pair of sawhorses with a board on top. But the older I get, the shorter the fuse on my patience gets, and while I have sawhorses aplenty, my general dissatisfaction with them grows.

Fixed-leg horses are heavy and clumsy to move around. The plastic folding ones are easier to use, but far less stable and sturdy. Some of my small trestle horses are better, but the stinking feet get snagged on anything and everything as I move them about, so I just leave them in the shop.

IDENTICAL QUADS. It's critical that the four panels be identical. These four stacked pieces are each 30" x 30", minus the saw kerf. Each corner is simply tacked with a finishing nail to keep them together during the cuts.

And for a lot of tasks two sawhorses are too many, and one is too few. But what if we had a sawhorse-and-a-half? A Workmate suffices sometimes, but it still is not exactly what I want.

With those limitations roiling my creative juices, I embarked on a path that eventually found me designing and building the "Butterfly" – a sturdy, lightweight, flexible and folding workholding option that is almost exactly the dreamt-of one-and-a-half sawhorses. I created my first prototype several years ago, and have tinkered with the concept and execution ever since to the point where I have it just where I want it.

Imagine a folding sawhorse, which is fine as far as it goes. But what if that single sawhorse had a pair of outriggers and could be transformed into two sawhorses on the same footprint? The Butterfly does exactly that.

As with most of my shop-accessory projects, this design is simple to construct with readily available materials and minimal tools. For the one built for this article, I used one sheet of ½"-thick Baltic birch plywood (my favorite sheet stock, and it should be yours too!), a circular saw, drill and a small handsaw to finish off the cuts, along with some ordinary hinges and metal stock from the local hardware store.

For the fabrication of the folding braces that hold the folding/expanding parts in place, I used metal bar stock, copper rivets (available at your local hardware store or online), a ball-peen hammer and a piece of railroad rail as my anvil when cold riveting the hinge pins on the folding braces.

As with most of these types of projects, you can tailor the dimensions and features to fit your own preferences. This Butterfly is simply one of several I have built to varying specifications.

Four Squares to Start

The starting point for this project was a full sheet of 60" x 60" plywood. Because the Butterfly requires four identical pieces of

AS A GROUP. Most of the cuts can be made with a circular saw and a straightedge. Large holes reduce the weight by a considerable amount, but keep in mind that removing material reduces the strength of the unit.

IN THIS CORNER. Finish the cuts with a handsaw. (You could, of course, use a jigsaw or reciprocating saw instead.)

material, you could simply cut the sheet into quarters like I did here and proceed just fine, yielding a unit that is about 30" high, 30" wide and 30" deep.

Once the four identical pieces are cut, tack them together for the second phase of the project as you lay out and cut vertical and horizontal cross members, and the attendant center cutout. This is a bit of a fussy part, because the cutout for the center yields panels that I use on top as a working surface. I wanted panels the width of the horses, so I needed two 15"-wide pieces for each wing of my Butterfly.

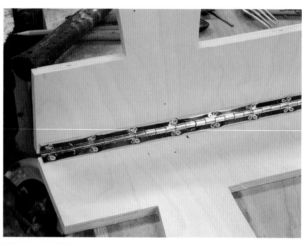

IN THE CENTER. A piano hinge inside the middle section allows the horse to open without any play.

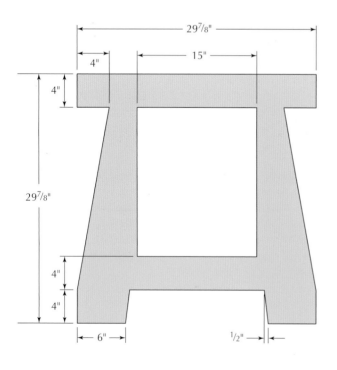

ELEVATION

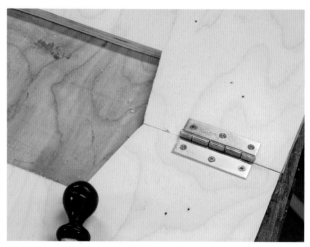

ON THE OUTS. Surface-mounted butt hinges allow the outer leaves to swing open. Gravity keeps the leaves in place when the Butterfly is used as a standard horse.

Cold Riveting

Cold riveting is a near-perfect and simple way to join two pieces of flat metal. Simply put, a rivet is a metal rod inserted into a same-sized hole that penetrates both pieces to be joined. The rod protrudes a little on each end (the protrusion should, ideally, be equal to half the diameter of the rivet), then the protruding rod ends are hammered into mushrooms, locking the assembly together.

If you do not have copper or brass rivets on hand, you can use either brass rod or brass machine screws from the hardware store. If you use machine screws,

make sure to file the threads off or the rivet will bind the brace pieces too tightly for them to fold easily. Cut the braces to the proper length with a hacksaw.

Before hammering the rivets, you should anneal them. Simply put them on a hot plate, turn it as hot as it can get and wait for the pieces to completely discolor to blue-grey. Let them cool before you use them. Insert the rivet into the drilled hole and using a hammer on an anvil, pound each end into a mushroom and you are done.

Using a clamped-on straightedge to guide the circular saw, followed by a handsaw, I cut the perimeter of the center void for each of the leg units. If you wanted, you could skip this step and leave each 30" x 30" piece whole. That results in a much stronger but much heavier Butterfly.

With the center panels cut out, lift the unit to decide how much more material – if any – you want to remove to achieve a desired weight. I made tapered cutouts along the vertical edges and foot cutouts at the bottom of all four elements to get a weight that suited my desires. If you want to remove even more weight, you can do as I did on an early prototype and remove stock along the edges using a hole saw.

With each of the four elements cut out, they are ready for the initial assembly. The tops of the two center pieces are joined with a piano hinge to make sure there is no racking in the finished unit. The two outside units are attached to the adjacent center sections at the feet with standard butt hinges.

Keep Your Distance

At this point you have a rough-assembled complete Butterfly. Fold it flat and on both front and rear edges, mark the halfway height; this is a critical measurement to fabricate and attach the folding braces.

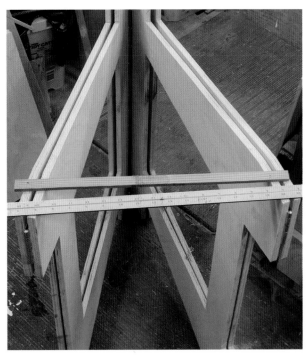

STAY PUT. After opening, the center section is splayed 15" and a piece of scrap is tacked in place to maintain that distance.

TRIED & TRUE. The whole assembly is placed on a flat surface and the upper edges are aligned to a single plane. With the pieces tacked together, the sizes of the brace parts can be determined.

Next, tack wooden strips to the center pair so the feet are splayed at your desired dimension. Flip the entire unit upside down on a flat surface, and splay the outside sections exactly the same as the feet. It is critical that you check the mock-up upside-down on a perfectly flat surface to make sure you have everything exactly configured.

Using the previously marked half-height dimension, measure and cut the necessary metal bar stock for making the folding braces. I prefer cold riveting for making the hinge pins of the folding braces (see "Cold Riveting" on page 13).

Braces & Tops

I take precise measurements with dividers to get the construction of the braces exact, mark the hole locations with a punch, then drill them out. The two holes that will be joined with a rivet are left

REPURPOSED. Use the cut-outs from the wings as a quick work surface when the need arises.

unmodified; the other two holes (the ends) can be countersunk for flathead screws or left unchanged if you use roundhead screws.

Once the braces are finished, you can simply screw them into the edges of the four folding units at the half-height mark. I like to screw the outermost brace ends first, then assemble the other end of the outer-unit braces and the end of the center-unit brace into the same hole, with the center brace on top of the outer brace.

You are now done building the basic Butterfly. The completed appliance is amazingly strong; this one holds several hundred pounds, as long as the weight is centered on the unit overall. I once loaded an early prototype with more than 1,000 pounds; it stood strong.

But for this iteration, I wanted to include a semi-integral "table-top" to place on the unfolded unit for a more solid working surface. My center cutouts worked great for this purpose, and they are easy to store. Using wooden tabs, the top panels are held in the voids of the four sections and, with the turn of the tabs, are easily removed to be used as needed.

RIVETED BRACES. The braces are made of ⅛"-thick x ½"-wide aluminum bar stock (or similar material) held together with rivets.

KEEPING TABS. The top panels are stored in the open area of the legs, retained by tabs that pivot on screws.

Chapter Three

Simple Sawbench

by Christopher Schwarz

Most first-time chairmakers are intimidated by the compound joinery used to fasten all the legs, stretchers, spindles and arms. The truth is, it can be quite complicated if you try to figure out everything using trigonometry. But if you take some lessons from other chairmakers (like I did more than 10 years ago), there are easy ways to design and build chairs without math.

So put away the scientific calculator and fetch some scrap pine, 12-gauge steel wire from the home center and needle-nose pliers. We're going to design and build a simple sawbench with five pieces of wood and compound angles.

What Is Rake, Splay & 'Resultant Angle?'

When chairmakers talk about the angles of chair parts, they use the terms "rake" and "splay" to describe them. Rake is the angle of the legs when you look at the chair from the side. The front legs rake forward; the rear legs rake back. Splay is the angle of the legs when you look at the chair from the front. Chair legs splay out.

I don't mess around with describing or measuring rake and splay much, except to explain it to other builders.

Instead, I use what is called the "resultant angle" – one angle that describes both the rake and splay. You can calculate this angle with trigonometry, but there is a simpler way to think about compound leg angles for those who consider mathematics a cruel master.

The resultant angle is not measured from the front or side of a chair. Instead of looking at a chair from the front or side, you look at the chair from a position in space where the leg doesn't appear angled at all.

If I've lost you, try this: Sit on the floor with a chair in front of you. Rotate the chair until the leg closest to you looks to be perfectly 90°. Imagine that one of your eyes has a laser in it and can shoot a line through the leg and onto the seat. That laser line is what chairmakers call a "sightline" – an imaginary line through the leg and onto the seat. Put a single bevel gauge on that imaginary line and you can position a leg in space with a single setting on a bevel gauge that is placed on your sightline.

Most plans for Windsor chairs include instructions for laying out the sightlines and the resultant angles for setting your bevel

ONE ANGLE. The bevel gauge is set to 15° and has been placed on the sightline on the underside of this sawbench. This "resultant" angle allows you to drill the holes for your legs with one line and one setting of your bevel gauge.

LEG LAYOUT. Here I've laid out the leg locations in this half-scale model of my sawbench.

GUIDED BY WIRE. The wire should be straight and strong enough that you can tap it into its hole on the underside of the model.

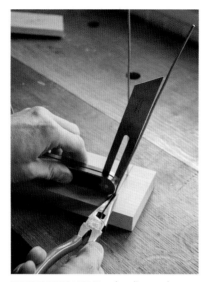

MAKE THE RAKE. Use the pliers at the base of the legs to bend them to 14° to match your bevel gauge.

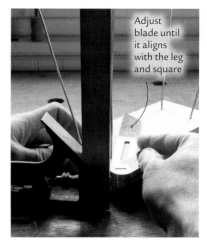

Adjust blade until it aligns with the leg and square

WHEN THE TOOLS ALIGN. Rotate the sawbench model until the leg looks vertical compared to your try square. Adjust the bevel gauge until its blade aligns with the leg and square. Hold your head still and you will be surprised by how accurate this is.

gauge. But what if you want to design your own chair? Or you want to build a table, desk or footstool using the same joinery?

Build a Model

When I design a chair, I make a simple half-scale model using scrap wood and bendable wire. This method helps me visualize how the parts will look when I walk around the chair. The model also gives me all my resultant angles and sightlines without a single math equation.

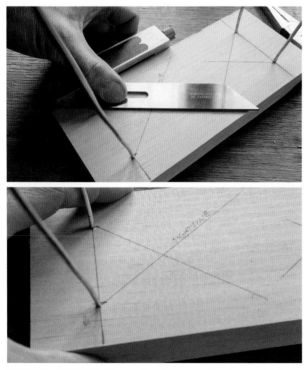

SEE THE SIGHTLINE. Use your bevel gauge to draw in your sightlines on the underside of the model. You are almost done.

I first learned this technique from Drew Langsner's "The Chair-maker's Workshop," a fantastic book. I then adapted his method to remove all math. Let's use it to design a sawbench.

Take a piece of ¾" pine and cut it to half the size of the finished sawbench. The finished top will be 2" x 7¼" x 17", so make your model ¾" x 3⅝" x 8½". Next, decide where you want the legs and lay out their locations on the model. Each leg is located 2½" from the end of the model and 1¾" from the edge. A lot of this is "by eye" so don't worry about it too much.

Now snip four pieces of 12-gauge wire to 10" long. (Note: You can also use wire coat hangers.) This wire will represent the legs of the sawbench. Drill a ⁵⁄₃₂" through-hole for each "leg" on your model and epoxy the wire into the hole.

Now comes the fun part. Set your bevel gauge to 7° using a plastic protractor. Look at the model directly from the end of the board. Let's call this the front of the sawbench. Use needle-nose pliers to bend the wire legs so they all splay out 7° from the top. Try not to manipulate the rake.

THE RESULT. You just found the resultant angle. Paired with the sightline, you can build these sawbenches with great ease.

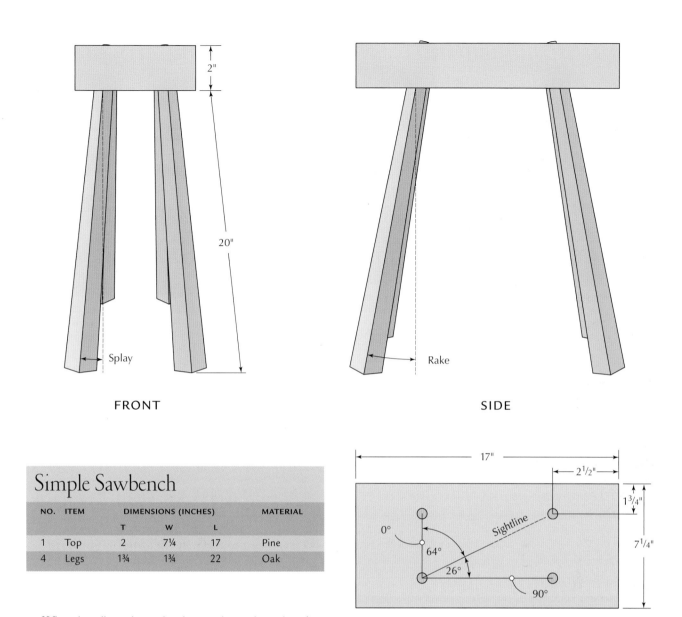

FRONT

SIDE

Simple Sawbench

NO.	ITEM	DIMENSIONS (INCHES)			MATERIAL
		T	W	L	
1	Top	2	7¼	17	Pine
4	Legs	1¾	1¾	22	Oak

TOP – UNDERSIDE LAYOUT

When they all match your bevel gauge, change the setting of the bevel gauge to 14°. This will be the rake. Look at the sawbench directly from its side and use your pliers to bend the legs to 14°. You might have to tweak things a bit so all the legs look the same.

Turn the model on its feet and look at the result. You will be surprised by how easy it is to spot angles that look wrong. Adjust the wires until they all look the same and the sawbench looks stable.

Find the Sightline & Resultant Angle

Turn the model back over. Place a try square on the bench with the blade pointing to the ceiling. Rotate the model until one of the legs appears to be 90° in relation to the square. Place the stock of your bevel gauge against the long edge of the model and push the blade of the bevel gauge until it appears to line up with both the leg and blade of your try square. (Hold your head still.)

Lock the bevel gauge. This is your sightline. Place the bevel gauge on the underside of the model. Butt it against one of the legs and draw a line. You have found the sightline (by the way, it's about 64°).

Now find the resultant angle. Unlock the bevel gauge and place the tool's stock on the sightline. Lean the blade until it matches the angle of the leg. Lock the gauge. That is your resultant angle – it should be about 15°.

Build the Sawbench

Building this quickie sawbench in a day will cement these concepts in your brain and give you a great workshop accessory. It also will introduce you to the basic ideas behind Windsor chair joinery.

I used poplar for the top and oak for the legs. You can use other species, but I recommend a soft species for the top and a hard species for the legs. The top is 2" x 7¼" x 17". Cut the four legs to 1¾" x 1¾" x 22" and make them into octagons, either with a plane or your table saw. Taper the legs so they are 1¼" square at their tops.

Now form the tenons on the tops of the legs. Rough in the tenon using a drawknife, or you can do this on the lathe. Each

TAPER THE LEGS. You don't have to taper the legs, but they sure look a lot less like broom handles when you do. I taper legs with jack and jointer planes.

SHAVE THOSE TENONS. A tapered tenon cutter makes this joint as easy as sharpening a (very large) pencil.

tenon should be 2⅞" long, 1⅛" in diameter at its base and taper to a little more than ⅝" diameter at the tip.

Now finish the shape with a ⅝" tapered tenon cutter. This inexpensive tool is available from Lee Valley Tools and works like a pencil sharpener.

Make the Top

Use your model to lay out the location of the legs on your real sawbench and draw in the sightlines (64°) using a bevel gauge. Then reset your bevel gauge to the 14° resultant angle. Clamp it to the sightline and your workbench.

Chuck a ⅝" auger bit in your brace and plant your feet perpendicular to your sightline. Put the tip of the bit on the location

of your leg mortise and tip the brace to match the resultant angle. Bore until the lead screw of the auger pokes through the other face of the seat. Remove the bit, flip the top over and finish the cut from the top of the sawbench.

Now ream this hole to a shape that matches the tenon. Lee Valley sells a matching reamer than can be used in a brace, electric drill or drill press. Ream the ⅝" holes until the tip of the reamer just fills the ⅝" exit hole on the top.

Assembly

Assign each leg to a mortise and number the legs and holes. You want the annular rings of each leg's end grain to run parallel to the grain of the top. So twist the legs in their mortises until this is the

READY TO BE BORED. Lay out the sightlines and leg locations on the underside of the top. I also drew in a centerline to confirm my sightlines and leg locations were consistent.

NICE RESULTANT. Use a spotter to help make sure you stay parallel to the blade of your bevel gauge. You'll outgrow a spotter eventually.

MATCHING TOOLS. The Lee Valley tapered tenon cutter and reamer have the same taper, which makes Windsor joinery a snap.

LOCKED. Wedging the joint from above makes this a long-lasting joint.

case and make a mark that allows you to get back to that position after you have added glue.

Remove the legs and saw a 1"-deep kerf in the top of the legs to hold an oak wedge. The kerf in each leg needs to be perpendicular to the grain of the top (and perpendicular to the annular rings of the leg's end grain) so you won't split the top when you drive the wedges in.

To assemble, paint the joinery surfaces with hide glue (it's reversible), and drive in the legs with a mallet. Then flip the sawbench over. Paint the wedges with glue and hammer them into the kerfs in your legs.

After the glue is dry, level the wedged joints. Then level the legs (a short video on leveling can be found at popularwoodworking. com/article/video-level-the-feet-of-a-chair-or-sawbench). I paint my sawbenches; they usually end up covered in paint eventually anyway as they make a great platform for finishing furniture.

That's really all there is to compound angles — the only math you'll do is counting all the additional things you can build with this skill.

Good Wood for Staked Furniture

Many woodworkers have limited access to green, rivable stock. So when I started building staked furniture such as these sawbenches, I began with the assumption that you will buy wood from the local lumberyard or the home center. That translates to legs from red oak and seats from poplar.

Tulip poplar is soft, cheap, difficult to rive and can be found in thicknesses up to 4" at most lumberyards. It's fairly easy to work with hand tools and is quite paintable. So it's perfect for a seat or a tabletop.

For the legs you need something hard, readily available and cheap – red oak. You can buy tons of it for little cash, and it's readily available in 8/4, which is perfect for the legs of staked pieces.

For the leg stock, look for straight grain on both the face and edge of the board. And the straight grain on the edges is more important than the grain on the face. If you can find a board with straight grain on its edges, buy it.

What about moisture content? If you work with green wood, you ideally want bone-dry legs and slightly moist stock for the seat or top. That way the seat will shrink on the legs and tighten the joint.

If you buy your stock from the lumberyard, you might not have much choice about the moisture content of your wood. So don't worry too much about it. Buy your red oak. Cut it into 24" or 30" lengths and let it sit until you are ready to use it. You want the leg stock to be dry.

Right before you build your staked project, buy the poplar and get to work. Whether it's dry or wet, things will be OK. Just make sure the legs are at equilibrium before you get busy.

You might have other options in your area. Seats can be basswood, white pine or cedar. Legs can be white oak, maple (soft or hard), hickory, ash or anything harder than the seat and tough enough to take a hard knock with a mallet.

But don't let the available species stop you from building something you need. It didn't stop people during the last 500 years or so.

Supplies
Lee Valley Tools • leevalley.com or 800-871-8158
1 ⅝" Tapered tenon cutter, #05J61.09, $39.00
1 Large standard reamer, #05J62.01, $26.50
Prices correct at time of publication.

Under-$250 Workbench

by Christopher Schwarz

I've hauled my grandfather's workbench across snow-covered Appalachian mountains, down narrow stairwells and into a dirt-floored garage that should have been torn down during the Eisenhower administration. I've built a lot of good stuff on that bench, but there came a time to retire the old horse.

For starters, the bench was too low for the way I work. And the top was pockmarked with three different shapes and sizes of dog holes. I had become fed up with the tool tray. The only thing it seemed designed to hold was enough sawdust for a family of gerbils. So I needed a new bench, but there's no way I was going to spend $1,200 to $1,400 for a high-quality bench from Hoffman & Hammer or Ulmia.

Enter Bob Key from Georgia. His off-the-rack pine workbench design has become a bit of a staple of the woodworking community. Inspired by his design, I spent a week reading up on benches and poring over woodworking catalogs. And after a lot of figuring I came up with a simple plan: Build a bench for less than $175 – that was 2001; today the same bench will cost you around $250.

Believe it or not, I came in under budget and ended up with a bench that is tough, sturdy and darn versatile. I made a few compromises when choosing the hardware to keep the cost down, but I designed the bench so that it can later be upgraded with a nice tail vise. However, I made no compromises in the construction of the top or base. You can dance on this bench.

Let's Go Shopping

OK friends, it's time to make your shopping list. First a word about the wood. I priced my lumber from a local Lowe's. It was tagged as Southern yellow pine, appearance-grade. Unlike a lot of dimensional stock, this stuff is pretty dry and knot-free. Even so, take your time and pick through the store's pile of 12-foot-long 2x8s with care

to get the best ones possible. You can hide a few tight knots in the top, but with luck you won't have to.

Here's the story on the hardware. The bolts, nuts and washers are used to connect the front rails to the two ends of the bench. Using this hardware, we'll borrow a technique used by bed makers to build a joint that is stronger than any mortise and tenon. The Bench Dog and Wonder Dog will keep you from having to buy an expensive tail vise. Using these two simple pieces of hardware, you can clamp almost anything to your bench for planing, sanding and chopping. The traditional face vise goes on the front of your bench and is useful for joinery and opening jars of peanut butter.

Preparing Your Lumber

Cut your lumber to length. You've probably noticed that your wood has rounded corners and the faces are probably less than glass-

When you glue up your top, you want to make sure all the boards line up. Lay down your glue and then clamp up one end with the boards perfectly flush. Then get a friend to clamp a handscrew on the seam and twist until the boards are flush. Continue clamping up toward your friend, having your friend adjust the handscrews as needed after each clamp is cinched down.

smooth. Your first task is to use your jointer and planer to remove those rounded edges and get all your lumber down to 1⅜" thick.

Once your lumber is thicknessed, start working on the top. If this is your first bench, you can make the top, then throw it up on sawhorses to build the base. The top is made from 1⅜" x 3⅜" x 70" boards turned on edge and glued face-to-face. It will take 10 of your 2x8s, trimmed to 70" in length and ripped to 3⅜" wide, to make enough pieces for the top. Build the top in stages to make the task more manageable. Glue up a few boards, then run the assembly through the jointer and planer to get them flat. Make a few more assemblies like this, then glue all the assemblies together into one big top.

8	2 x 8 x 12' Southern yellow pine boards @ $9.67 each	77.36
8	⅜" x 16 x 6" hex bolts @ 60 cents each	4.80
8	⅜" x 16 hex nuts @ 5 cents each	.40
16	5⁄16" washers @ 5 cents each	.80
1	Veritas Bench Dog (see Supplies for ordering information)	15.95
1	Veritas Wonder Dog (see Supplies for ordering information)	39.50
1	Veritas Front Vise (see Supplies for ordering information)	96.50
	Total Cost plus tax and shipping.	$235.31

When you finally glue up the whole top, you want to make sure you keep all the boards in line. This will save you hours of flattening the top later with a handplane. See the photo above for a life-saving tip when you get to this point. After the glue is dry, square the ends of your assembled top. If you don't have a huge sliding table on your table saw, try cutting the ends square using a circular saw (the top is so thick you'll have to make a cut from both sides). Or you can use a hand saw and a piece of scrap wood clamped across the end as a guide.

Build the Base

The base is constructed using mortise-and-tenon joinery. Essentially, the base has two end assemblies that are joined by two rails. The end assemblies are built using big 1"-thick, 2"-long tenons. The front rails are attached to the ends using 1" x 1" mortise-and-tenon joints and the 6"-long bolts.

Begin working on the base by cutting all your pieces to size. The 2¾"-square legs are made from two pieces of pine laminated together. Glue and clamp the legs and set them aside. Now turn your attention to cutting the tenons on the rails. It's a good idea to first make a "test" mortise in a piece of scrap so you can fit your tenons as they are made. I like to make my tenons on the table saw using a dado stack. Place your rails face down on your table saw and use a miter gauge to nibble away at the rails until the tenons are the right size. Because pine is soft, be sure to make the shoulders on the edges 1" wide on the upper side rails. This precaution will prevent your tenons from blowing out the top of your legs.

Now use your tenons to lay out the locations of your mortises. See the photo on page 26 for how this works. Clamp a piece of

Drilling the ⅜" holes for the bolts is easier if you do it in this order. First drill the holes in the legs using your drill press. Now assemble the leg and front rail. Drill into the rail using the hole in the leg as a guide (left). Remove the leg from the rail and continue drilling the hole in the rail. The hole you drilled before will once more act as a guide. You still need to be careful and guide your drill straight

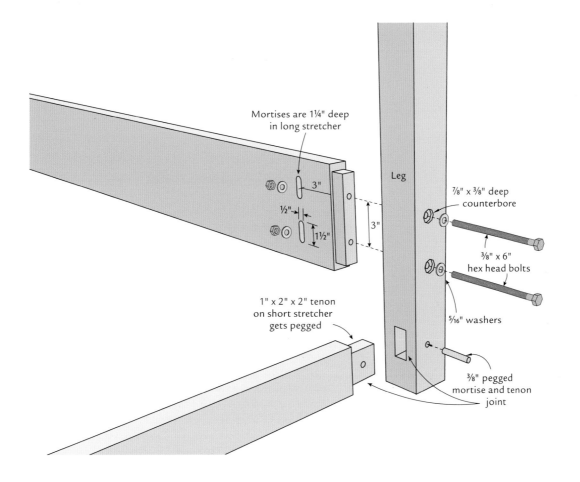

Mortises are 1¼" deep in long stretcher

3"

½"

1½"

Leg

⅞" x ⅜" deep counterbore

3"

⅜" x 6" hex head bolts

5⁄16" washers

1" x 2" x 2" tenon on short stretcher gets pegged

⅜" pegged mortise and tenon joint

After you cut your tenons, lay them directly on your work and use the edges like a ruler to mark where the mortise should start and end (left). Use a 1" Forstner bit in your drill press to cut overlapping holes to make your mortise (bottom, left). Now square up the edges of the mortise using a mortise chisel and a small mallet (below).

The Pleasure & Pain of Pine

Southern yellow pine is cheap, but you probably know that it likes to twist, cup, wind and bow – everything but corkscrew. There's a way to prevent this, and it's a simple trick that will help reduce warping in all your projects.

First, after you cut your pieces to size, store them on edge with about an inch of space between them. One of the major reasons pine bows is that it's not completely dry (surprise). When you stack it flat, one side is exposed to the atmosphere and the other is not. As a result, one side dries faster than the other and the board bends. Leave a pine board alone for a night like this and the next morning you'll probably have a bowl.

Here's another tip. When you get set to assemble your top, do it all in one day. Surface all your boards and glue them up as fast as you can. If a pine board is in a lamination, it's much less likely to bow because it has other boards that may cancel out its tendency to warp.

scrap to your drill press to act as a fence and chain-drill the mortises in the legs. Make your mortises about $1/16"$ deeper than your tenons are long. This will give you a little space for any excess glue.

Once you've got your mortises drilled, use a mortise chisel to square the round corners. Make sure your tenons fit, then dry-fit your base. Label each joint so you can reassemble the bench later.

Bed Bolts

There's a bit of a trick to joining the front rails to the legs. Workbenches, you see, are subject to a lot of racking back and forth. A plain old mortise-and-tenon joint just won't hack it. So we bolt it. First study the diagram on page 25 to see how these joints work. Now here's the best way to make them.

First chuck a 1" Forstner bit in your drill press to cut the countersink in the legs for the bolt head. Drill the countersinks, then

The mortises in the front rails are also made on the drill press. Make them 1¼" deep to make sure you can get a washer in there. If you can't, try clipping an edge off of the washer.

Supplies

Lee Valley Tools • leevalley.com or 800-871-8158
Bench Dog #05G04.01, $15.95
Wonder Dog #05G10.01, $39.50
Large Front Vise #70G08.02, $96.50
Prices correct at time of publication.

Drilling your dog holes may seem like hard work using a brace and bit. It is. However, you get an amazing amount of torque this way – far more than you can get with a cordless drill. Sadly, I had cooked my corded drill, so this was my only option.

chuck a ⅜"-brad-point bit in your drill press and drill in the center of the counterbore through the leg and into the mortise.

Now fit the front rails into the leg mortises. Chuck that ⅜" bit into your hand drill and drill as deeply as you can through the leg and into the rail. The hole in the leg will guide the bit as it cuts into the rail. Then remove the leg and drill the ⅜" hole even deeper. You probably will have to use an extra-long drill bit for this.

OK, here's the critical part. Now you need to cut two small mortises on each rail. These mortises will hold a nut and a washer and must intersect the ⅜" holes you just drilled. With the leg and rail assembled, carefully figure out where the mortises need to go. Drill the mortises in the rails as shown in the photo. Now test your assembly. Thread the joint with the bolt, two washers and a nut. Use a ratchet and wrench to pull everything tight. If your bench ever wobbles in your lifetime, it's probably going to be a simple matter of tightening these bolts to fix the problem. Remember to tell this to your children.

Base Assembly

This bench has a good-sized shelf between the front rails. Cut the ledgers and slats from your scrap. Also cut the two cleats that attach the top to the base. Now sand everything before assembly – up to #150-grit should be fine.

Begin assembly by gluing up the two end assemblies. Put glue in the mortises and clamp up the ends until dry. Then, for extra strength, peg the tenons using ⅜"-thick dowel. I had some lying around. If you don't, buy the dowel at the hardware store and add $1 to your bottom line.

Screw the ledgers to the front rails. Make sure they don't cover the mortises for the bed bolts, or you are going to be in trouble. Now bolt the front rails to the two ends (no glue necessary). Rub a little Vaseline or grease on the threads first because after your bench is together you want to seal up those mortises with hot-melt glue. The Vaseline will ensure your bolts will turn for years to come.

Screw the cleats to the top of the upper side rails. Then drill oval-shaped holes in the cleats that will allow you to screw the top to the base. Now screw the seven slats to the ledgers.

Finishing the Top

Before you attach your top, it's best to drill your dog holes and attach the vise. Lay out the location of the two rows of dog holes using the diagram. I made a simple jig to guide a ¾" auger bit in a brace and bit. The jig is shown in action in the photo on page 27.

Now position your vise on the underside of the top and attach it with the bolts provided by the manufacturer. This Czech-made vise is of surprising quality, with a heavy-duty Acme-thread screw. The only downside to the vise is you are going to have to make your own wooden face. I must confess I didn't have enough wood left over from my 2x8s to make the face. So I made it from a small piece of scrap from another project. You'll need to drill three holes in the wooden face so it fits over the bars, but this is pretty self-evident

when you pull the vise out of the box. All the European benches I've seen have a bead cut on the edges. I'm not one to argue with tradition, so I used a beading bit in a router table to cut beads on mine, too.

Make the vise's handle from a length of 1"-diameter oak dowel. My handle is 20" long, which is just the right length to miss whacking me in the head at every turn. I'm a tall guy, so you might want to make yours a bit shorter.

You are now almost done. It's necessary to flatten the top. Use "winding sticks" to determine if your top is flat.

Winding sticks are simply identical, straight lengths of hardwood. Put one on one end of the top and the other on the far end. Now crouch down so your eye is even with the sticks. If your top is flat, the sticks will line up perfectly. If not, you'll quickly see where you need work. Use a jack plane to flatten the high spots. Then sand your top and rag on a couple coats of an oil/varnish blend on the base and top.

With the bench complete, I was pleased with the price and the time it took, which was about 30 hours. If you want to spend a little more you can customize it by building a cabinet beneath the bench and adding a leg jack for planing the edges of long boards (see "Upgrade Your Bench" on page 52).

Under-$250 Workbench

NO.	ITEM	DIMENSIONS (INCHES)			COMMENTS
		T	W	L	
1	Top	3	27	70	
4	Legs	2¾	2¾	35	
2	Front rails	1⅜	7	49	1" TBE
2	Upper side rails	1⅜	7	21	2" TBE
2	Lower side rails	1⅜	3	21	2" TBE
2	Ledgers	1⅜	1⅜	47	
7	Slats	1⅜	3	18½	
2	Cleats	1⅜	1⅜	17	

TBE= Tenon, both ends

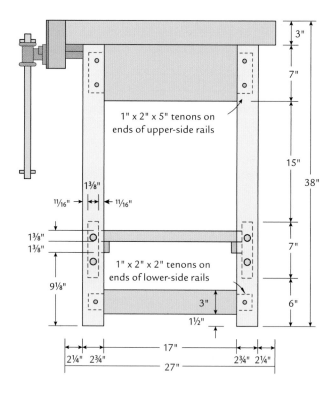

1" x 2" x 5" tenons on ends of upper-side rails

1" x 2" x 2" tenons on ends of lower-side rails

3"
7"
15"
38"
7"
6"
1⅜"
11/16"
11/16"
1⅜"
1⅜"
9⅛"
3"
1½"
17"
2¼" 2¾"
2¾" 2¼"
27"

PROFILE

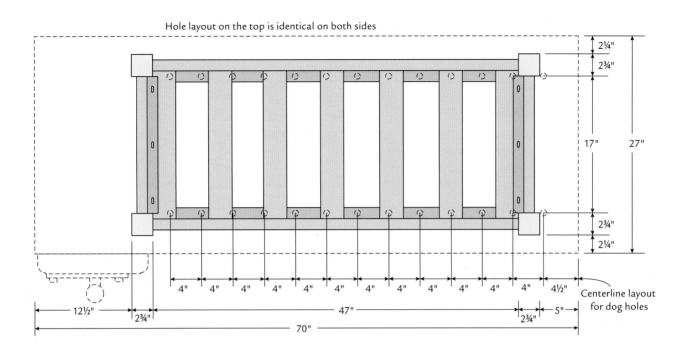

Hole layout on the top is identical on both sides

2¼"
2¾"

17" 27"

2¾"
2¼"

4" 4" 4" 4" 4" 4" 4" 4" 4" 4" 4" 4½"

Centerline layout
for dog holes

12½" 2¾" 47" 2¾" 5"

70"

PLAN

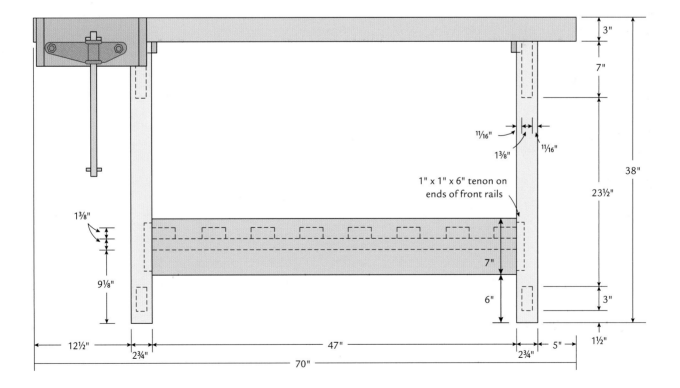

3"

7"

11/16"

1³⁄₈"

11/16"

38"

1" x 1" x 6" tenon on
ends of front rails

23½"

1³⁄₈"

9⅛"

7"

6"

3"

12½" 2¾" 47" 2¾" 5" 1½"

70"

ELEVATION

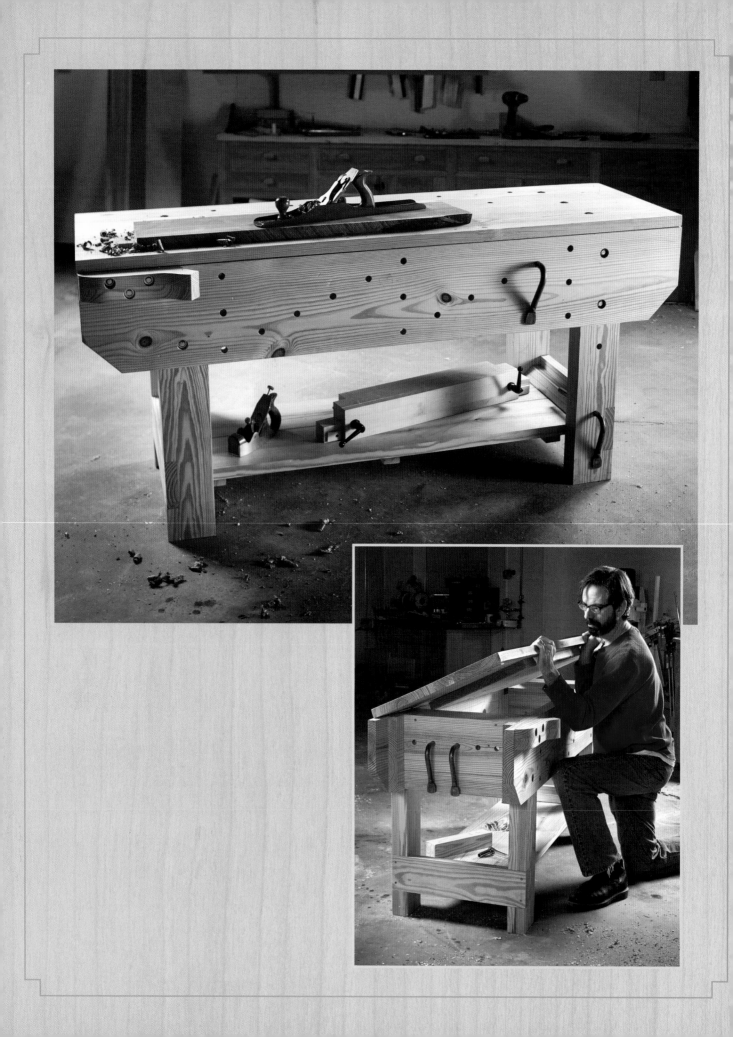

Chapter Five

Knockdown English Workbench

by Christopher Schwarz

Many knockdown workbenches suffer from unfortunate compromises.

Inexpensive commercial benches that can be knocked down for shipping use skimpy hardware and thin components to reduce shipping weight. The result is that the bench never feels sturdy. Plus, assembly usually takes a good hour.

Custom knockdown benches, on the other hand, are generally sturdier, but they are usually too complex and take considerable time to set up.

In other words, most knockdown workbenches are designed to be taken apart only when you move your household. When I designed this bench, I took pains to ensure it was as sturdy as a permanent bench, it could be assembled in about 10 minutes and you would need only one tool to do it.

The design here is an English-style workbench that's sized for an apartment or small shop at 6' long. It's made from construction lumber and uses a basic crochet and holdfasts for workholding. As a result, the lumber bill for this bench is about $100. You'll need four 2" x 12" x 16' boards and one 1" x 10" x 8' board.

I used yellow pine for this bench, but any heavy framing lumber will do, including fir, hemlock or even spruce.

The hardware is another $75. The supplies list notes high-quality hardware from McMaster-Carr; you could easily save money by doing a little shopping or assembling the bench with hardware that is slower to bolt and un-bolt.

About the Raw Materials

The core of this workbench is ductile iron mounting plates that are threaded to receive cap screws. This hardware is easy to install and robust. The rest of the hardware is standard off-the-rack stuff from any hardware store.

MOUNTED FOR WORK. The ductile mounting plates are easy to install and durable.

No matter where you buy your lumber, make sure it has acclimated to your shop before you begin construction. This workbench is made up of flat panels, so having stable wood will make construction easier and will reduce any warping that comes with home-center softwoods.

When I bring a new load of lumber into my shop, I cut it to rough length and sticker it. I have a moisture meter that tells me when the wood is at equilibrium. If you don't have a moisture meter, wait a couple of weeks before building the bench. Also, if the end grain of any board feels cooler to the touch than its neighbors, then that board is still wet-ish and giving off moisture. So you might want to give that stick some more time to adjust.

This workbench is made up of five major assemblies that bolt together: two end pieces, two aprons and a top. Each assembly needs some cutting and gluing. Let's start by building the legs.

Glued-up Legs

The joinery for this workbench is mostly glue, screws and a few notches. All those joints are in the two end assemblies. Each end assembly consists of two legs made by face-gluing two boards together. The act of gluing these two boards together creates a notch for the bench's aprons.

So begin making the end assemblies by gluing the 5½"-wide leg parts together for each of the four legs. If you don't own clamps, glue and screw these parts together, then remove the screws after the glue has dried. If you own clamps, I recommend sprinking a pinch of dry sand on the wet layer of glue between the laminations to prevent the pieces from shifting during the clamping process.

While the glue in the legs is drying, turn your attention to the aprons.

Laminated Aprons

Like the legs, the front and rear aprons of the workbench are made by face-gluing two parts together to thicken the piece and create notches for the other assemblies.

Each apron consists of a 2x12 glued to a smaller 1x10 piece. The 2x12 is the exterior of the workbench. The 1x10 makes notches for the legs.

The length of the 1x10 is the distance between the left legs of the bench and the right legs. In this 6' workbench, the 1x10 is 45" long. If your bench is longer, make these parts longer.

FOUR LEGS GOOD. By gluing a short piece and a long piece together, you create a thick leg and the notch for the workbench's apron.

APRONS AT WORK. Here you can see the 2x12 apron glued to the 1x10 interior piece. The legs will then butt against the 1x10.

CAN'T MISS. By drilling these holes while the pieces are together, you ensure they will mate up again.

MOUNTING PLATES. Here is how the mounting plates look when they are installed. First you tighten the bolts, then you screw the mounting plate down. This way you can't miss.

Glue and affix a 1x10 to its 2x12 – and make sure the smaller piece is centered on the length of the larger. I used glue and nails to put these parts together. Any combination of glue, screws and nails will do.

Once the aprons are assembled, you can then clip the corners of the aprons if you like. The 45° corners are cut 4" from the ends of each apron with a handsaw. The next step is to use the heavy-duty ductile hardware to bolt the legs and aprons together.

Hardware Install

Clamp a leg to one of the aprons, making sure the leg is snug against the notch created by the apron's 1x10. Now lay out and drill the counterbore for the washer and the clearance hole for the bolt's shaft. The clearance hole should go all the way through the apron and leg. The counterbore should be deep enough to hold the head of the bolt, the washer and the lock washer.

Now lock the leg and apron together with the hardware. Thread the bolt through a lock washer and then a washer. Push the bolt through the clearance hole. Spin a ductile mounting plate onto the bolt on the other side.

Snug up the mounting plate, then tighten the nut with a socket wrench. Once both bolts are snugged up on the leg, you can permanently install the mounting plates with screws.

Repeat this process with the other three legs. When you are done you will have two aprons with their legs attached.

Beefy Benchtop

One of the downsides to many English workbenches is that the top is springy because it is thin or unsupported from below. The traditional solution was to add "bearers" under the benchtop.

These cross members ran between the front apron to the rear apron. And while they do make the benchtop stouter, I have never liked these tops as much as I like a simple thick benchtop.

The top surface of the benchtop is made from 2x12s that have been edge-glued to create a flat panel. This benchtop is 22½" wide

LEGS & APRONS. With the legs and aprons bolted together, you can glue up the parts for the benchtop.

EASY & ACCURATE. I use aluminum angle pieces for winding sticks. I also use them as edge guides for my circular saw. Clamp the aluminum angle to your benchtop and make your cut.

LEG UP. With the bench temporarily assembled like this, you can fit the pieces between the legs so they match the space available.

CAN'T MISS II. With the top plate between the legs, you can put each stretcher on with screws (skip the glue because this is a cross-grain construction).

because it is made from two 2x12s. You can make it narrower if you like – an 18"- to 20"-wide bench is stable enough for handwork.

Glue up your two planks for your benchtop and cut the top to its finished width and length.

It might be tempting to glue on the second layer of 2x12 to make the benchtop its final thickness. Resist. It is easier to first attach the aprons, legs and thin top. Then, once you finish building the end assemblies, you will know the exact size of this second top piece and exactly where it will go without measuring.

Feet in the Air

This next step ensures that the end assemblies will be the correct size for the width of your top. Assemble the bench upside down on

sawbenches. Clamp the aprons to the top and push things around until the legs are square to the underside of the top and the aprons line up with the top all around.

Once you have everything clamped as you like it, you can fit the pieces for the end assemblies that go between the front legs and the back legs. There is a top plate that is the same width as the legs, plus a top stretcher made from a 2x12 that fits between the front apron and the rear apron.

Cut these pieces to fit. Then wedge the top plate pieces between the legs and screw the stretchers to the legs.

With the top stretchers screwed to the legs, you can take the bench apart, then glue and screw the top plates in place. Don't for-

Knockdown English Workbench

NO.	ITEM	DIMENSIONS (INCHES)			MATERIAL
		T	W	L	
4	Legs (interior)	1½	5½	32½	Yellow Pine
4	Legs (exterior)	1½	5½	21¼	Yellow Pine
2	Aprons (exterior)	1½	11¼	72	Yellow Pine
2	Aprons (interior)	¾	10	45	Yellow Pine
1	Benchtop (exterior)	1½	22½	72	Yellow Pine
1	Benchtop (interior)	1½	18	45	Yellow Pine
2	Top stretchers	1½	11¼	19½	Yellow Pine
2	Top plates	1½	5½	16½	Yellow Pine
2	Lower stretchers	1½	5½	22½	Yellow Pine
4	Glue blocks	1½	11¼	2½	Yellow Pine
1	Planing stop	2½	2½	12	Yellow Pine
1	Crochet	3	4	12⅜	Yellow Pine
1	Shelf	1½	16½	53	Yellow Pine
2	Cleats	2	2	16½	Yellow Pine
3	Battens	1½	2	14½	Yellow Pine

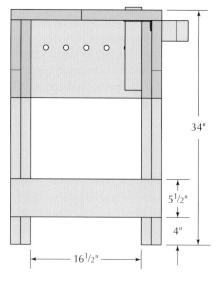

34"

5½"

4"

16½"

PROFILE

get to glue the edge of the top plate to the face of the top stretcher. There is a lot of strength to be found there.

The last bit of work is to attach the lower stretchers to the legs. These stretchers are in a notch in each leg. Cut the notch with a handsaw and clear the waste with a chisel. Then screw and glue the lower stretchers into their notches.

Reassemble the bench's base so you can get the top complete.

The Top (& Details)

With the base assembled, level the top edges of the aprons and the end assemblies so they are coplanar – that's the first step toward a flat benchtop.

I dressed these parts with a jointer plane and block plane and checked my work with winding sticks and a straightedge.

Before you put the top on the base, I recommend one little addition at this stage. I attached glue blocks – for the lack of a better

AN END, ASSEM-BLED. I know this is an odd construction, but it works. And once you see it, you'll get it. Here you can see the finished end assembly with the lower stretcher ready for trimming and screwing.

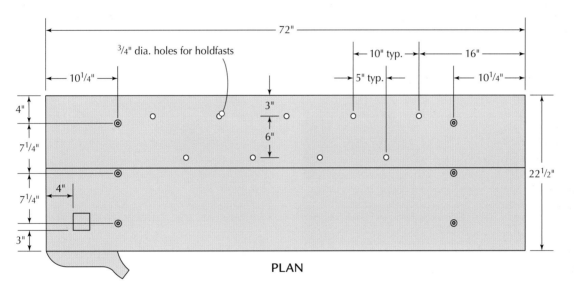

PLAN

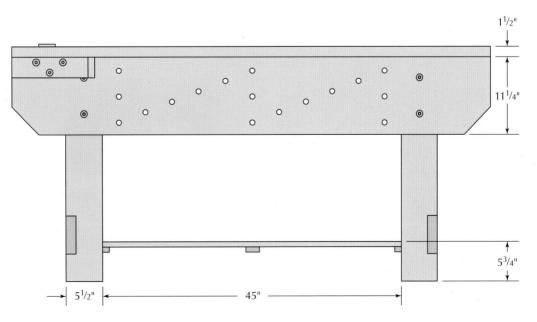

ELEVATION

FLAT MAKES FLAT. If your bench base is twisted, your benchtop will be twisted. It pays to get all the base bits in the same plane.

BENCH, FLATTEN THYSELF. Traverse the underside of the benchtop with a jack plane to get the surface fairly true.

word – to the aprons so the end assemblies would be captured. You can see in the photo above (top) that I used an offcut from a 2x12 and oriented the grain sympathetically with the apron. This five-minute upgrade makes the bench easier to assemble and a bit stouter.

Now you can flatten the underside of the benchtop by using the bench's base for support.

Put the benchtop on the base and plane the underside of the top flat with a jack plane – don't worry about flattening the top of the benchtop. A couple of F-style clamps on the bench base will keep the top in place during this operation.

Test your benchtop by flipping it over and showing it to the workbench's base. When the two parts meet without any rocking, you are done. Clamp the benchtop in place with the worksurface facing up. Now install the bolts, washers and mounting plates through the top and the top plate of the end assemblies. Do this in the same way you attached the legs to the aprons.

Now flip the assembled bench over. You now can see the precise hole where the second benchtop piece should go. Glue up a panel using 2x12 material and cut it to fit that hole exactly. Glue and screw it to the underside of the benchtop. Then lift the workbench

Viseless Workholding

You have probably used benches with vises your entire woodworking career. A face vise and tail vise are pretty much the way to go, right?

Maybe. Maybe not.

Once you get the hang of it, viseless workholding becomes very fast and can be liberating and fun. Many of these techniques are quite useful, even if you have a vise on your bench. I find them useful for the entry-level person on a budget as well as for the seasoned woodworker seeking to expand his or her options.

Let's look at how to accomplish some of the more common tasks at a bench: planing faces, edges and ends of boards; crosscutting and ripping; and sawing a couple of joints.

— Mike Siemsen

END GRAIN. A bench hook can be used as a simple shooting board for longer or wider boards; the plane rides on the bench-top.

DOVETAIL CHOPPING. Stacking the parts to be chopped saves the need to reset the holdfast individually for each workpiece.

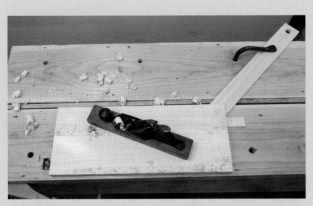

FACE PLANING. Face planing is accomplished by using a planing stop in combination with either battens or a doe's foot. A holdfast keeps the doe's foot in place at the corner of the workpiece to push it against a toothed planing stop. The wedge under the workpiece corner keeps a high corner from rocking. Plane toward your stop and the battens, and don't drag your plane on the return stroke, or the board will pull away from the stop. Flip the doe's foot over if the angle is wrong for a holdfast hole.

EDGE PLANING. Here are two positions for edge planing: One board is in the crochet and supported by pegs (in holes in the apron) and a batten; the other is supported by the benchtop and held against the planing stop. If the pegs are too far apart, place a batten on the pegs and place the edge of your stock upon that. If the workpiece is narrow and flexes under the plane, or doesn't reach above the benchtop with the pegs in their highest position, plane the board against the planing stop on the benchtop. If there are hollows under the board, place wedges in them to keep the board from flexing away from the plane. If the board tips over, you are not planing with even pressure. End grain can be planed in the same manner, but to avoid splintering, plane almost to the corner, then flip the workpiece and finish planing.

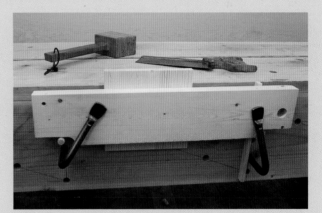

DOVETAIL SAW CUTS. Secure the workpiece against the apron with a thick batten held flush to the benchtop with two holdfasts, and supported by two pegs in the apron's holdfast holes. I like to take a scrap of stock the same thickness as the material being dovetailed and put it to one edge of the chop. I place my holdfast just to the inside of the scrap and give it a good whack. This will keep that end of the chop fixed so that I need only to loosen the other holdfast when changing out parts to be worked.

TENONS. Tenoning can be accomplished with the material in the crochet, angled against a peg and held with a holdfast. Angle the board away from you and saw the corners, reverse the board to saw the opposite corners, then square across the bottom. Cut the shoulders in the bench hook (or at the end of the bench using pegs and a holdfast).

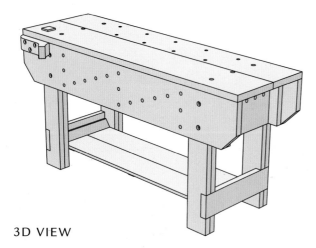

3D VIEW

BORING FOR STRENGTH. I put three bolts through each assembly. This keeps things flat. Yellow pine doesn't move much, so I allowed for only a little expansion and contraction by making my clearance holes 1/16" larger than the diameter of my bolts.

base off the benchtop and clamp the top pieces together for extra bonding power.

When the glue is dry, use a block plane to bevel the mating surfaces so they will slide together easily during assembly.

Holes & Holding

You just made a table. Now you need to make it a workbench. To do that you need to add three things: a crochet, a planing stop and holdfast holes. The holdfast holes restrain your work on the benchtop and front apron. The crochet is for edge planing. The planing stop is for lots of things. Let's make the holdfast holes first.

To lay out the holdfast holes on the aprons, draw two or three rectangles on the aprons between the positions of your bench legs. Two rectangles for a 6' bench; three for an 8' model.

Connect two corners of each rectangle with a diagonal line. Then use dividers to equally space six holes from corner to corner on the diagonal lines. Then divide the vertical ends of each rectangle into three using your dividers.

Drill ¾"-diameter through-holes at each of these locations. These holes in the aprons are great for supporting work from below, especially when edge-planing or dovetailing.

Now lay out the holdfast holes on the benchtop. My preference is to have two rows of holdfast holes on the benchtop (you can always add more later). One row is about 3" from the back edge of the benchtop. These should be spaced every 10" to 16" depending on the reach of your holdfast. Then make another row of holdfast holes about 6" in front of your back row. These should be spaced similarly, but these holes should be offset from the first row, as shown in the drawings and photos.

Be sure to drill some holdfast holes in the legs – both to store holdfasts and to support large work, such as passageway doors. Hold off on drilling any additional holdfast holes until you really need them.

The Planing Stop

The traditional planing stop is a workhorse. I push workpieces against it to saw them, plane them, stick moulding on them, you name it. The stop is a piece of dense wood (yellow pine is dense enough) that is friction-fit into a mortise in the benchtop.

First make the mortise, then make the planing stop to fit.

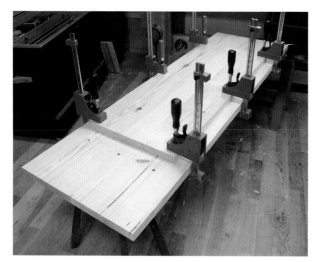

OVERKILL. After gluing and screwing the second benchtop piece in place I also clamped things together while the glue dried.

APRON HOLES. Here I'm drawing the diagonal lines for the holdfast holes in the aprons. Many people use wooden pegs in the aprons instead of holdfasts. Both solutions defy gravity just fine.

SQUARE HOLE. This is a great first mortise for a beginning wood-worker. Take your time in squaring up the walls.

THE HOOK. You can bolt your crochet on. Some early accounts indicate it was nailed on. You probably could get away with glue alone.

The mortise for the planing stop is right in front of the end assembly and typically 3" or so in from the front edge of the benchtop. This planing stop is 2½" x 2½" x 12" – a fairly traditional size.

Lay out the mortise on both faces of the benchtop. Then bore out most of the waste with a large-diameter bit. Finish the walls with a chisel. It pays to check the walls so they are perfectly square to the benchtop.

Then plane the planing stop until it is a tight fit in the mortise and it requires mallet blows to move it up and down. Some planing stops also have a toothy metal bit in the middle that helps restrain your work. You can add that later if you like. It can be a blacksmith-made stop, a piece of scrap metal screwed to the top of the planing stop or even a few nails that are driven through the stop so their tips poke out.

Le Crochet

For this workbench I decided to make a crochet that looks exactly like the one in Roubo's "l'Art du menuisier." But to be honest, I don't think the shape matters much. I've used a lot of different shapes and they all seem to work fine as long as they are vaguely "hook-shaped."

I made this crochet from scraps. I glued them together, then shaped the hook on the band saw, finishing it up with rasps.

I attached the crochet with two lag screws and one cap screw, which was backed by a ductile mounting plate. This allows me to remove the crochet from the apron. As you might notice in the illustration on page 38, and in the photo above right, the crochet slightly interferes with one of the cap screws through the apron. You can avoid this by altering the shape of your crochet or moving the hole for the cap screw.

A Shelf if You Like

I always like having a shelf below my bench to store bench planes and other assemblies. I haven't included the shelf in the calculation for buying materials, so you'll need some extra wood and screws to get the job done.

The shelf is simply a panel that rests on cleats that are glued and screwed to the lower stretchers of the end assemblies. You can also screw some battens to the underside (and/or top) of the shelf to help keep it flat.

The only thing holding the shelf in place is gravity.

And Finish

You don't want to make your bench too slippery, so stay away from film finishes (or French polish). I recommend using little or no finish. For most workbenches, I usually just add a coat of boiled linseed oil. You can use an equal blend of oil, varnish and mineral spirits or just leave the wood bare.

In the end, this really is a remarkably sturdy bench. Most people who use it cannot even tell that it is designed to be knocked down. It is only after they notice the cap screws in the benchtop that they suspect anything.

Supplies

McMaster-Carr • mcmaster.com or 330-995-5500
15 Ductile mounting plates for ⅜" x 16 threaded rod
#11445T1, $1.83/ea.
15 High-strength steel cap screws, ⅜" x 16 thread
#92620A636, $9.95/pack of five.
Tools for Working Wood • toolsforworkingwood.com
or 800-426-4613
1 pair Gramercy Holdfasts, #MS-HOLDFAST.XX, $34.95
From any retailer:
Plain steel ⅜" flat washers (at least 15)
No. 10 x 1" slot-head screws (for attaching the mounting plates)
No. 8 x 2½" wood screws to assemble the ends
No. 8 x 1¼" wood screws for attaching the interior apron bracing (you'll need about 20)
Prices correct at time of publication.

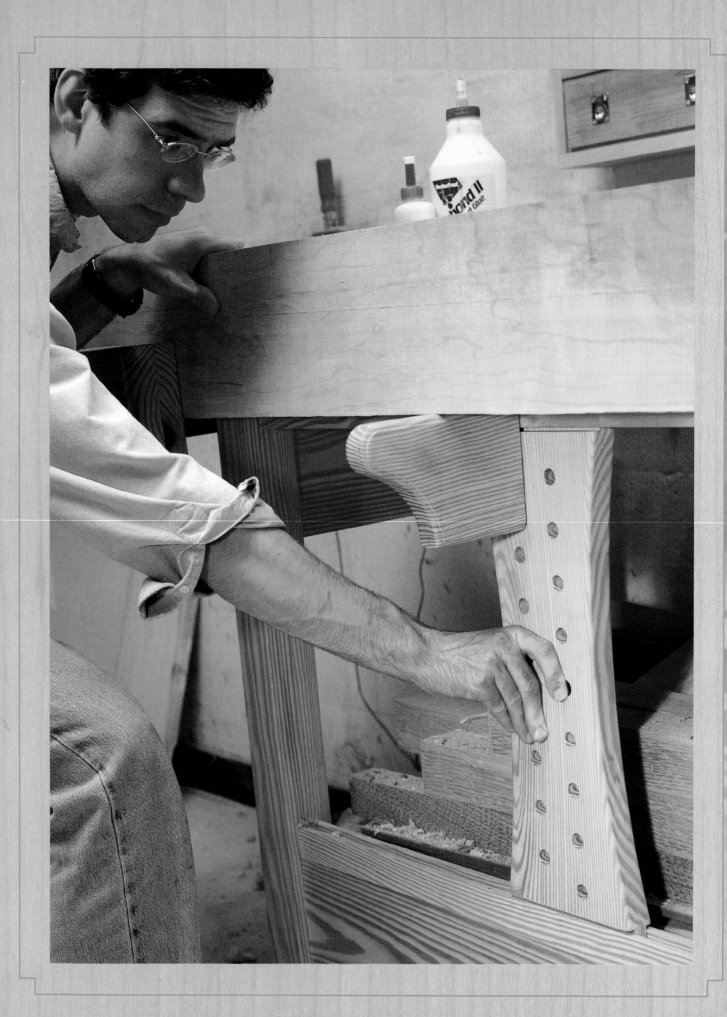

Chapter Six

Bench Deadman

by Christopher Schwarz

There are few clamping jobs that are more difficult than trying to secure something big so that you can work on its edge. Mortising a large door for a hinge is a common situation. Cleaning up the long edge of a board you just band sawed is another.

These problems are quickly and easily solved with $10 and by taking a lesson from 18th-century joiners. A common feature on older benches is what's called a sliding deadman. This contraption works with your face vise to support work that is long, wide or both long and wide. I adapted mine from a sketch of a deadman by Graham Blackburn that was featured in his excellent book "Traditional Woodworking Handtools" (The Lyons Press). This particular version is sized to fit our "Under-$250 Workbench" on page 22, though you can easily cut the rails and the sliding deadman to fit your bench.

After you determine the proper dimensions for all your parts, begin by cutting your pieces to rough size. Cut a ⅜"-deep x ⁹⁄₁₆"-wide groove in the center of a long edge of each rail. Use a dado stack in your table saw, a straight bit in your router or a plough plane to cut the groove.

Before you cut the curves on the deadman itself, bore the ⅝"-diameter holes through the part for the ledge. I bored two staggered rows of holes; each hole is 2" down from the one above it. The topmost hole is located so that when the ledge is in place in the deadman, it lines up with the rails on my face vise.

Cut the ½"-long x ½"-thick tenons on both ends of the deadman. The tenons are slightly thinner than the width of the grooves they ride in. Now cut the deadman to shape. The long edges are curved in ⅞" so they are easy to grasp when the deadman is resting against your bench's legs. Round over the long edges of the deadman to make it friendly to grasp. I used a ¼" roundover bit in a router.

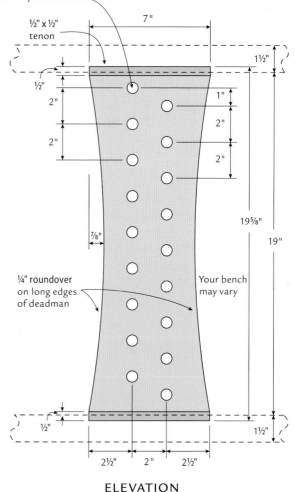

Align top hole with rails of your face vise

½" x ½" tenon

7"

1½"

½"

2"

2"

1"

2"

2"

19⅝"

19"

⅞"

¼" roundover on long edges of deadman

Your bench may vary

½"

1½"

2½"

2"

2½"

ELEVATION

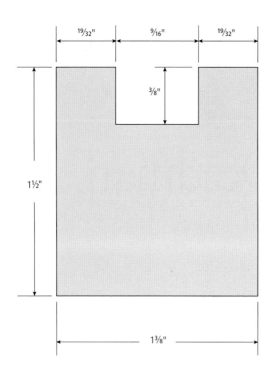

RAIL DETAIL

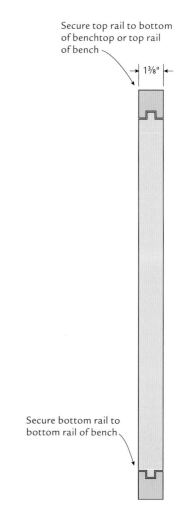

Secure top rail to bottom of benchtop or top rail of bench

Secure bottom rail to bottom rail of bench

SECTION

Trim your rails to the proper length and install them. Screw one rail to the bottom rail of your bench using four #8 x 2" screws. Don't use glue; you want to be able to remove the rail for later adjustments or repairs. Now put the top rail and deadman in place and line them up with the bottom rail. Using screws, secure the top rail to the underside of your bench's top, or to the top rail of your bench — if you have one. Wax the grooves in the rails. The deadman should slide back and forth with minimal effort.

Now make the ledge. You could simply use a dowel. I chose to make one a little fancier. Bore a 1¼"-deep hole in one end for the ⅝" dowel and glue it in place, again making sure that when the ledge is inserted into the top hole, it lines up with the rails on your face vise. You might need to sand your dowel to fit the holes in the deadman. I used a ¼" beading bit in a router to shape three edges of each side of the ledge. Finish your deadman to match your bench.

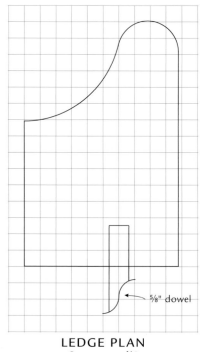

LEDGE PLAN
One square = ½"

Bench Deadman

NO.	ITEM	DIMENSIONS (INCHES)			MATERIAL	COMMENTS
		T	W	L		
2	Rails	1⅜	1½	47	SYP	
1	Deadman	1⅜	7	19⅝	SYP	½" TBE
1	Ledge	1⅜	4⅞	7½	SYP	
1	Dowel	⅝ dia.		5		

TBE = Tenon on both ends; SYP= Southern Yellow Pine or Equivalent

Chapter Seven

Moxon's Ingenious Bench Vise

by Christopher Schwarz

If you cut dovetails by hand, then I'm sure you're aware of the other part of your anatomy that is involved: your back.

Bending over rows of tails and pins all day is murder when you try to stand up straight. Several people have come up with solutions, including a cute mini-bench that you park on your full-size bench to raise your work. Other woodworkers have built benches with higher benchtops that are designed just for hand-joinery.

Of course, like most things in woodworking, someone had already come up with the solution several centuries ago.

'Mechanick Exercises'

Joseph Moxon wrote the first English-language book on woodworking titled "The Mechanick Exercises" in 1678. In it he showed many of the tools used by the contemporary joiner, from the workbench down to the dividers.

In one part of his book he discusses the "double-screw" vise. It looks like a twin-screw vise with two jaws that has been affixed to the front of a workbench.

But the text discusses how the vise can also be clamped down to the top of the workbench.

When that piece of information sunk in, I got excited and built a prototype. After a few revisions, here is what I came up with.

This vise solves a lot of problems that we joiners have. It allows you to hold stock of almost any size (mine holds up to 24⅛"-wide material) with an incredible grip. More so, it raises your work above your benchtop surface. The vise as shown is 6" high, so the top edge of the vise is 39" from the floor. The board I've clamped in the vise is 44" off the floor and is as stable as something clamped between two boulders. What does that mean?

No more stooping to saw dovetails, tenons or other joinery.

And because the vise is portable, that means I can:

1. Put the vise wherever I want on the bench – the end, the back edge, wherever.

2. Remove it when I don't need it and hang it on the wall – most woodworkers don't need a twin-screw vise every day.

TAP THEN TAP. Place the front jaw on the rear jaw. Drop your Forstner in the hole. Tap it with a hammer. Then drill the hole in the rear jaw and tap that.

3. Leave it unclamped on the benchtop, and use it like a giant handscrew clamp (Peter Follansbee at Plimoth Plantation hipped me to this function).

The vise is quite easy to build – I used some scraps. The only other key piece of shop equipment is a 1½" wooden thread box and tap, which is available at many suppliers for less than $50.

Tap the Jaws

The first step is to cut the 1½"-diameter clearance holes in the front jaw. Position the holes so you'll have 24⅛" between them. Then center the front jaw on the rear jaw and clamp them together. (Note: The front jaw is wider than the rear jaw so that it is easier to line up the rear jaw with the front edge of your benchtop.)

Drop a 1½" Forstner bit into each hole and tap the end with a hammer – this transfers the centerpoint of the hole to the rear jaw.

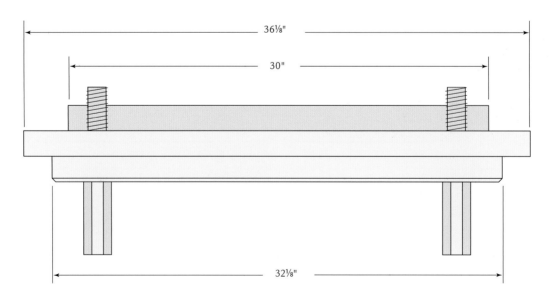

36⅛"

30"

32⅛"

PLAN

TWO SCREWS FROM ONE STICK. The two vise screws are made from one octagonal piece. Turn down the middle. Cut the piece in half. Thread the round sections.

Unclamp the jaws and drill 1⅜" holes though the rear jaw. Then use your tap to tap the holes in the rear jaw (a little linseed oil or a non-drying vegetable oil makes a good lubricant).

Turn & Thread the Screws

The vise's screws are made from 2" x 2" walnut. I planed a 25"-long section to an octagon then chucked that in the lathe. I turned the middle 14" down to just a shade less than 1½". Then I crosscut the piece, ending up with two 12½"-long handles.

Clamp a vise screw with the round section facing up and use your threadbox to thread the round section. Test the results in the rear jaw. If the screw squeaks or doesn't turn freely, adjust the cutter in the threadbox so it cuts slightly deeper.

Add the Rear Brace

The vise will be more stable if you glue a rear brace on the backside of the rear jaw, which will increase the surface area that contacts your bench. Glue and clamp the rear vise in place.

Add some details if you like. I chamfered the front edges of my front jaw and the ends of the vise screws. I applied a couple coats of an oil/varnish blend finish. I also glued on a layer of suede to the inside face of the front jaw, which improves the vise's grip even more.

I've been testing the vise for more than three months (and I made versions for co-workers and friends). If you cut dovetails, I think this vise is well worth making. Your back will thank me.

PROFILE

Profile dimensions: 1¾", 1¾", 5", 2", 2", 1¾"

Joseph Moxon's Double-screw Vise

NO.	ITEM	DIMENSIONS (INCHES)			COMMENTS
		T	W	L	
2	Bench screws	2	2	12½	7" of screw is 1½" dia.
1	Front jaw	1¾	6⅛	32⅛	
1	Rear jaw	1¾	6	36⅛	
1	Rear brace	1¾	2	30	

Chapter Eight

Flattening Your Workbench's Top

by Christopher Schwarz

L ike any tool or machine, a workbench requires accessories (jigs, fixtures, appliances) and occasional maintenance to actually do anything of great value. A bench without a bench hook is a dining table. A bench with a cupped work surface is an exercise in bewilderment and wasted effort.

There are a variety of ways to go about flattening a workbench top, including some that are patently nuts. But before I march down that list of your options, I ask: Does the top need to be flat?

Whenever I'm in an old barn, workshop or even an antique mall, I can't resist poking around the guts of any old workbenches I find. When my wife and I take the kids on a hayride, I end up in the chicken house checking out the 18th-century wooden screws on a face vise. When we visit living history museums, the kids are chasing the animals, and I'm asking the guy dressed as a cooper if I can poke around the undercarriage of his bench.

I've found little evidence that these benches were flattened regularly. Many of them bear toolmarks that are deep and of varying ages. I've seen benches that are so worn from use that the edges look as round as a pillow. One bench I saw in Columbus, Ohio, was so worn away in one spot that its 3"-thick top was less than an inch thick.

And when I check the 19th- and early 20th-century books, there's very little attention given to the workbench top. While there is detailed instruction on sharpening, tool maintenance and the act of building a bench, flattening its top isn't often listed as routine shop maintenance. At most, they'll note that the top should be flat.

There are several explanations for this:

1. Workbench flatness is overrated and a product of our modern obsession with granite surface plates and dial calipers.

IN THE RIGHT LIGHT. Move your bench so that one end points to a window. This makes it easier to read your winding sticks as you look for gaps underneath them and for alignment across their lengths.

2

LOOK FOR WARP. My winding sticks here are 36"-long aluminum angle. Place one winding stick at the far end of your bench and the other one about 24" away. Sight across them both, looking for high and low spots. Move the far winding stick to the other end of the benchtop and repeat.

3

CUP OR BOW? Now that I know the geography of the top, I'll drag one stick all along the top and watch the gap under the winding stick. This quick check confirms my suspicions about where the high spots are (and they are usually along the long edges of the top).

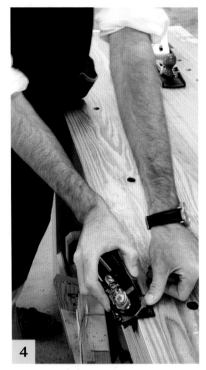

4

STOP SPELCHING. Before I get down to business, I'll cut a small chamfer ($\frac{1}{16}$" to $\frac{1}{8}$") on the long edges of the top. This will prevent the grain from blowing out (the British call this spelching) when I plane cross-grain.

5

IN MY CUPS. In general, my tops become cupped in use. So I remove the two high hills by working directly across the grain. In this instance the cup is slight, so I started with a jointer plane. If the cup is severe, start with a jack plane so you can take a thicker shaving.

6

ACROSS AND DOWN. Every stroke across the top should overlap the stroke before. The shavings will give up easily (though I am told that the iron will dull more quickly). Work from one end of the top to the other. Then back down. Repeat until the plane's cutter can touch the hollow in the middle.

7 DIAGONAL MAKES A DIFFERENCE. Work across the top diagonally now, overlapping your strokes as before. Take care at the starting corner and stopping corner – your plane's sole won't have much support. You can proceed with speed during the middle strokes.

8 AND THE OTHER WAY. Switch directions and work diagonally the other way across the top. Repeat these two types of passes until you can make shavings at every point in a pass.

9 FINISH PLANING. Now reduce your depth of cut and use your jointer plane along the grain of the top. Overlap your stokes and repeat your passes until you are getting full-length shavings.

2. Early woodworkers would use "planing trays" – a disposable workshop appliance that attached to the bench and allowed woodworkers to plane cabinet-scale parts at a variety of angles.

3. Or a flat workbench was so important to those who handplaned panels and furniture components that its flatness was a given.

I don't have the answer, but I suspect that all three are true to some degree. If you've ever done any handwork on a bench that was cupped, bowed or twisted, then you know that it's not a good way to work. The downward pressure from a handplane (particularly wooden-bodied planes) can bend your work into a low spot in the bench. When using long planes in particular, a low spot will prevent you from ever planing the board flat.

You can use small wooden wedges under your stock to support it and prevent it from bending into a low spot on your bench, but the problem is that you will have difficulty knowing when your board is flat. A workbench top that is fairly flat is also a fair way to gauge the flatness of other boards.

Two Solutions for Tops

So my recommendation is that if you can wield a handplane (even just enough to be trouble), then you should either use a planing tray or strive to keep your top fairly flat. You can overdo this. It's not necessary to flatten the top using methods that involve a machin-

ist's straightedge and feeler gauges. And I would ward you away from methods that use a router that runs on a carriage suspended over your bench. I've watched people do this, and it is a lot of trouble to build these devices.

I think there are two smart paths: Learn to use a jointer plane (flattening a workbench top is the best practice for this) or remove your benchtop and take it to a cabinetshop that has a wide-belt sander.

(Side note: Some workbench designs can be flattened using home woodworking machines. One such design has a benchtop that is made of two thick 10"-wide slabs with a 4"-wide tool tray screwed between them. Simply remove the screws and run each 10"-wide slab through your portable planer. Reassemble! Side, side note: I dislike tool trays, a.k.a. hamster beds.)

I can hear the workbench purists squirming from where I perch. Won't sending a workbench top through a wide-belt sander embed it with grit that will mar the workpieces of future projects? Not in my experience. Once you dust off the top and put a finish on it, such as an oil/varnish blend, the grit becomes part of the finish.

Plus, even if there is a little #220-grit in my benchtop, that fine grit is a lot kinder to my workpieces than what else gets embedded in my bench during my normal work: bits of dried glue, dyes, pigments and occasional stray metal filings.

FOR THE OBSESSED. You don't have to smooth-plane your benchtop, but it's good practice with a large laminated surface. You can begin smooth-planing with the grain; there is no need for cross-grain or diagonal strokes.

10

11

12

13

CROSS-GRAIN SHAVINGS. When working across the grain, this is what your shavings should look like. Take the heaviest cut you can manage and keep your handplane under control.

DIAGONAL SHAVINGS. Full-length shavings taken at 45° will look like thick ribbon. Shoot for a thickness of .005", or perhaps a bit more.

FOR THE OBSESSED II. If you smooth-plane your benchtop, set your tool to take a shaving that is .002" or less. You can take even more if your top is behaving and it is a mild wood.

14

WIPE ON, WIPE OFF. Rag on two coats of an oil/varnish blend. When everything is dry, a coat of wax will help your top resist glue, but it will make it slippery (a bad thing – hand-tool users don't want their stock sliding everywhere).

Flatten it With a Handplane

Because I don't have a wide-belt sander, I prefer to use a handplane to do the job. Once you do this a couple times, you'll find that it's a 30-minute job – and a lot less lifting than carting a top across town. The first time I ever tried to flatten a benchtop with a handplane (years ago) I was 100 percent successful, and I just barely knew what I was doing.

Flattening a benchtop is like flattening a board on one face. First you remove the high spots. These high spots could be at the corners or there could be a hump all along the middle (though I have never had one of these in my benchtop). Find the high spots using two winding sticks – parallel lengths of hardwood or aluminum angle that are longer than your bench is wide.

Mark any high spots in chalk or pencil and work them down with a bit of spirited planing using a jack, fore or jointer plane set to take an aggressive cut and equipped with a cambered iron. Get things close. Check your results with your winding sticks.

Fetch your jointer plane and work the entire top using diagonal strokes that overlap. Repeat that process by going diagonally back the other way across the top. After each pass, your shavings will become more and more regular. When your shavings are full length, your top is flat (enough). Now plane the entire top with the grain

and use slightly overlapping strokes. It should take two or three passes to produce regular full-length shavings. You are finished. So finish it with some oil/varnish blend and get back to work.

The pictorial essay that illustrates this chapter should help you visualize the process. My digital camera codes each photo with the time it was taken. The first photo was snapped at 10:46 a.m. By 11:44 a.m. I was done. And remember: I'd stopped to take photos about the process, and each photo had to be illuminated with our photographic lights. I think the photography took longer than the actual work.

BEFORE

AFTER

Chapter Nine

Upgrade Your Workbench

by Christopher Schwarz

I hate to say it, but no matter how much time and money you spent building or buying your workbench, it's probably not as useful as it should be. Like adjustments to a new table saw or handplane, there are a number of things everyone should do to tune up their bench. Also, there are several simple improvements that will make your bench perform feats you didn't think were possible.

Most of these upgrades are quick and inexpensive. All of them will make your woodworking easier, more accurate or just plain tidier.

1 Improve Your Topography

Flattening your benchtop regularly is like changing the oil in your car. It's a routine step that will save you headaches down the road. A flat top is essential to accurate work for three reasons:

• When planing, sanding or routing a board, you want your work to rest firmly against your bench; a flat benchtop helps keep your work in place.

• A flat top will divine whether your workpieces are cupped or bowed. If you ever want to remove the cup or twist from a door panel – a common malady – you must have a flat benchtop to know when your panel is finally flat.

• A flat top guides you as you assemble your projects. If you want your latest table, chair or cabinet to not rock, you have to make the legs or base all in the same plane. A flat bench will quickly point out your problems and the best solution.

So how do you flatten a benchtop? The simplest way is to run it through a big drum sander, which you can find in mid-sized cabinet shops. A couple woodworkers I know have paid about $50 for the privilege. The only downside is that you'll have some sanding grit embedded in your bench when it's all over, which can scratch your work in the future.

Winding sticks are the key to making sure a benchtop or tabletop is indeed flat. Check the top by moving the light-colored stick to different positions across the length of the bench and comparing the top edge of each stick.

Most of the hard work when flattening your top is handled by the No. 5 jack plane, which can take down high spots quickly. My bench always seems to dish in the middle (similar to a waterstone), so I begin by taking down the sides.

A No. 7 jointer plane's key asset is its length. Because of its length, the plane rides over the low spots and shears the high spots. Begin by working diagonally; don't worry about tear-out (left). When the top is flat from your diagonal passes, plane directly with the grain (above).

There is a way to flatten your bench at home by planing it with a router – once you build a somewhat complex carriage system that guides and holds the tool.

My way is faster. I flatten my benches with a No. 5 jack plane, an old No. 7 jointer plane, and a couple of sticks. The sticks are two pieces of plywood that measure ¾" x 2" x 36". (Aluminum angle also works well.) Traditionally called winding sticks, these will quickly determine if your bench is flat and where it's out of whack.

First place one of the winding sticks across one end of the bench. Then lay the other stick across the bench at various places along the length of the top. Crouch down so your eye is level with the sticks to see if their top edges are parallel. If they are, that area is flat. If they're not, you'll see where there are high spots.

Old-time winding sticks were made using a stable wood, such as mahogany, and were sometimes inlaid with ebony and holly on the edges (a black wood and a white wood) so you could easily see the difference. I prefer plywood because it's dimensionally stable and cheap. If you need contrast between your sticks, I highly recommend "ebony in a can" (black spray paint).

Mark all the high spots directly on your bench and start shaving them down with your jack plane. Continually check your work with your winding sticks. (For more on these sticks, see "Keep Your Winding Sticks in Focus" at right.)

When the top is reasonably flat, fetch your No. 7 plane. First plane the top diagonally, moving from corner to corner. Then come back diagonally the other way. Do this a couple times until you're taking shavings at all points across the top. Finally, plane the length of the bench. Start at the front edge and move to the back edge. When it looks good, check it with the winding sticks.

2 A Deadman Lends a Hand

One of the trickiest operations is working on the narrow edge of a board or door. Securing the work is the No. 1 problem. The traditional solution is what's called a sliding deadman. I installed the one shown here in an afternoon and now I wonder how I ever got by without it.

Because the deadman slides across the front of the bench, you can accommodate all lengths of work. And because the ledge can

While flattening the top is the most important upgrade, a close second is the sliding deadman. This clever bit of engineering will allow you to immobilize doors easily.

A leg jack is great for clamping long work, and it takes only about 20 minutes to add to your bench. There are fancier ways to do this, but none is more effective.

be adjusted up and down, you can hold narrow boards or even entryway doors. With the help of your face vise, you can immobilize almost anything with this rig.

I added the deadman by screwing two rails to my bench that each have a groove milled in one long edge. The deadman itself has a slightly undersized tenon on each end that allows it to slide in the grooves. See details and full instructions for constructing a deadman in Chapter Six.

3 Add a Leg or Bench Jack

While I consider the sliding deadman to be the cat's meow, there are simpler ways to support oversized work at your bench.

If you do a lot of work on big doors, a leg jack is probably the best bet for you. Basically you bore ¾"-diameter holes every 4" up the front leg of your bench that's opposite your face vise. (For example, if your vise is on the left side of your bench, bore the holes in the right leg.) Chamfer the holes (see the next section on dog holes for directions) then insert a ¾"-diameter dowel in one of the holes. You're in business.

This simple bench jack excels at clamping boards that are 8" wide or narrower. Like the leg jack, this is a quick upgrade.

Keep Your Winding Sticks in Focus

When using winding sticks, one of the difficulties is trying to keep both sticks in focus when they are 6' away from each other. If one of the sticks is blurry it's difficult to tell if they are in line with each other.

The solution comes from the world of photography. Take a piece of thin cardboard – I use the stuff from the back of a notebook. With your brad awl, punch a small hole (¹⁄₃₂" or so) in the center of the cardboard. Crouch down in front of your winding sticks and look at them through the hole. They should both be in focus.

In a camera, when you close the aperture (also called the F-stop), more of the picture is in focus. The same principle works with your eye. If you close the aperture that light passes through, more of what you see will be in focus.

As a practical matter when doing this, check both ends of the sticks by moving your eye left to right, not your head. It's easier to get a reading on your sticks this way.

The disadvantage of this jack is that it supports only long work. To hold shorter work, you need to add a second kind of jack to your bench – a bench jack.

For your bench jack, you'll bore the ¾"-diameter holes across the front edge of your workbench – every 4" or so should be sufficient. Make the holes about 2" deep and chamfer their rims.

Next get a 2" length of ¾" dowel. To create a ledge for the board to rest on, your best bet is to buy an L-shaped piece of steel from your local hardware store. This item usually has screw holes already bored in it and is used for reinforcing corners.

Screw this L-shaped steel to the end of the dowel. This jig now will allow you to hold narrow boards of almost any length in place so you can work on the edge.

4 Add Bench Dogs

A good system of bench dogs and dog holes makes routine operations easier and impossible tasks a cake walk. And retrofitting a bench with round dog holes is quick and simple.

I like to have at least two rows of dog holes running down my benchtop that are spaced 4" apart. On some benches, I've had the dog holes line up with the dogs on my tail vise so that I can clamp things between my tail vise and any dog hole on the bench. But even if you don't have a tail vise you can unlock the power of the dog hole with a product called the Wonder Dog from Lee Valley.

The Wonder Dog is essentially a mini-vise that slips into any ¾"-diameter dog hole. It allows you to apply pressure in any direction, which is great for clamping round or other irregularly shaped pieces for sanding or planing.

To drill the dog holes, your best bet is to make a jig like the one shown below (top right). Also grab a ¾" auger bit and a corded drill.

Clamp the jig to your bench and drill the hole all the way through the benchtop. Use a slow speed. After you drill each hole you need to chamfer the rim to keep from ripping up your benchtop when you pull out a dog. The easiest way to do this is with a plunge router.

Chuck a 45° chamfer bit that has a ¾" bearing on its end in your plunge router. Insert the bearing into the dog hole, turn on the router and plunge straight down, making a ⅜"-deep cut.

5 Add a Tail Vise

If you've got just one vise it's almost always on the front (sometimes called the face) of your bench. A tail vise (located on the end of the bench) is an extremely useful upgrade. The retractable metal dog on most vises allows you to clamp really long workpieces to your bench between the vise's dog and a dog in the benchtop. It's also just plain handy to have a second vise.

When choosing a tail vise, you have three good options:

If you can't afford a tail vise, these Wonder Dogs make many clamping chores easier. With two Wonder Dogs and bench dogs you can clamp odd-shaped material.

This gizmo works like a primitive doweling jig. Mark lines on your top where you want your dog holes. Clamp this jig to your bench and line it up with your marks. Drill away using a corded drill. Chances are you'll cook a cordless drill.

Chamfering your dog holes prevents you from tearing out the grain when you remove a stubborn dog.

A tail vise, such as this Veritas, is a luxury we all deserve. Since adding one to my bench at home, shown here, I've found myself using it far more than a face vise.

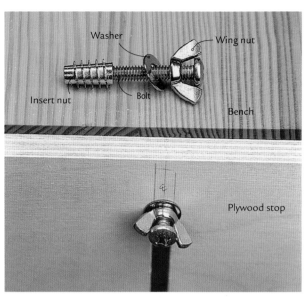

The key to the planing stop is the hardware. Here you can see how the ¼" x 20 screw-in insert nut, 1¼"-long bolt, ¼" x 20 wing nut and ¼"-hole washer are assembled.

• You can buy a traditional quick-release metal vise with a retractable dog for between $65 and $150. It's easy to install.

• You can buy a front-vise screw kit that you just add wooden jaws to. This option can be a bit cheaper (about $70) but requires more labor. The advantage to this vise is that you can add dog holes to the top or front edge of the wooden vise faces.

• You can buy an expensive specialty vise that will do things your face vise won't. The Veritas twin-screw vise ($239 - $249) gives you a huge tail vise that can be used for clamping or holding almost any flat work. Or you can buy a patternmaker's vise ($220 - $550) that excels at holding irregular objects at any angle. Both of these are expensive, but worth it.

6 Add a Planing & Sanding Stop

Many woodworkers clamp their work down when they don't have to. In many cases, gravity and the force of your tool will do the job.

A planing stop is essentially a lip on the end of your bench that can be adjusted up and down. When you're going to plane your work you merely put the wood against the stop and plane into it. The force of gravity plus the direction you are pushing your tool holds the work in place.

The same concept works for belt sanding. Just remember which way the sander spins. The front of the sander should point away from the stop. Otherwise the machine will shoot your work across the room, easily puncturing any styrofoam cooler in its path. Don't ask me how I know this.

The most versatile planing stop is a piece of ½"-thick plywood that is as long as your bench is wide. A couple wing nuts, bolts

If you use a handplane, you really should invest $6 and an hour of your time to make this planing stop. It is the most versatile stop I've ever used and works great for thick or thin stock.

and washers allow you to position and fix the stop up and down, depending on the thickness of your workpiece.

The hardware is readily available at any home center. The part that is driven into the bench is sold as a ¼" x 20 screw-in insert nut or threaded insert. To install it, first drill a ⅜"-diameter hole in the end of your bench. Coat the hole with epoxy and drive the insert in slowly using a (usually metric) hex wrench. Then thread a 1¼"-long bolt through a ¼" x 20 wing nut and a ¼"-hole washer.

The stop itself is plywood with two stopped slots that measure ⁵⁄₁₆"-wide. Make the slots long enough so your stop can go below the edge of your bench.

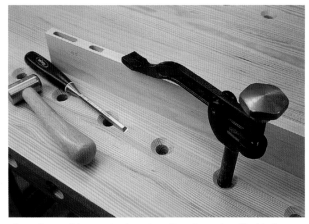

The Veritas Hold-Down is a joy. It's well-engineered and holds the work with astonishing pressure. I won't cut dovetails without it.

This stop allows you to plane wood of almost any thickness with ease. Unscrew the wing nuts, adjust the stop where you want it and tighten the wing nuts to hold the stop in place.

7 Add a Holdfast

Sometimes you need to hold a board on your bench so you can work on its end, such as when you're chiseling out the waste between dovetails. Nothing is as quick or efficient at this job as a quality holdfast.

A holdfast is essentially a hook that drops into a hole in your bench. You tighten it with a screw or rap it with a mallet to lock the work to your bench.

There are three major types that are worth purchasing. The Veritas Hold-Down is the Cadillac of the bunch ($85). It drops easily into any ¾" hole in your bench and is tightened by turning a screw on the top. I've used this holdfast every day for five years and has never let me down.

The second option is more economical. Glass-filled nylon hold-fasts are cheap ($12.50 a pair from Lee Valley Tools), but you have to reach under your benchtop to operate them.

The third type is a metal hook. Rap the top to tighten it and rap the back to release it. All of the versions I've seen in catalogs are cast metal and don't work well for me. My fellow hand-tool enthusiasts recommend forged holdfasts, which are handmade by blacksmiths. It's worth asking around in your area if there's a blacksmith who will do this work for you. Expect to pay about $30, maybe a bit more.

8 Add a Sharpening & Finishing Tray

While some people might accuse me of just being fastidious, there are sound reasons to protect your bench from sharpening slurry and finishing materials.

Sharpening slurry is made up of bits of metal and abrasive that will dig into your bench and later get embedded in your work. And finishing materials (dyes, stains and glazes in particular) can rub off on your work for weeks or years if they spill on your bench.

That's why a tray with a low lip is ideal for typical sharpening and finishing jobs. I make my trays from inexpensive plywood with the lip made of ¾"-thick scrap pieces — plus glue and screws. The best thing about the tray is that it drops into two dog holes, so

Never sharpen or finish on your bench without protecting the top. The slurry and stain will dig into your work and sully the wood you place on top of it. This simple tray drops into the dog holes in the top (no clamps) to contain your mess.

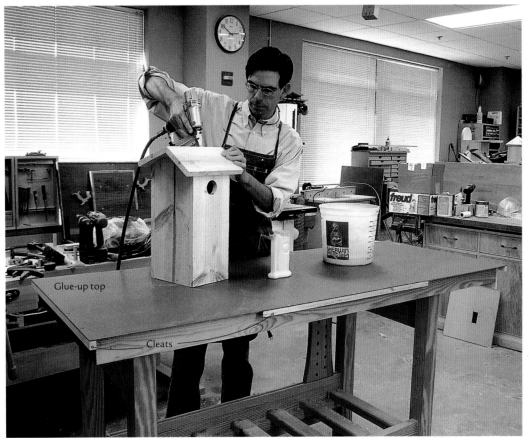

Glue-up top

Cleats

Until I can afford my 3,000-square-foot dream shop, I have to assemble projects on my bench. This cover keeps my benchtop like new. Make sure the cleats that keep the top in place don't interfere with your vises.

there's no need to clamp it in place. This makes the tray especially good for sharpening because the tray stays put as you work.

9 A Top Just for Gluing

Not all of us have the luxury of a separate bench for assembly, so I end up constructing most of my furniture right on my bench – both at work and at home.

Getting glue on the bench is a big problem most woodworkers face. Yellow glue, which is mostly water, isn't good for your top because you're introducing moisture in places where it has spilled. And dried glue can easily mar your work.

So I have a removable top that fits right over my benchtop for gluing chores. It's made using ⅛"-thick hardboard (available at your local home center store) and four cleats that keep it securely in place on the benchtop.

Why not use newspaper or a blanket? Well, newspaper makes a lot of waste, and is slow and messy. Blankets, if not perfectly flat on your bench, can actually introduce a little twist in your glue-ups. If you don't want to make a hardboard glue-up top, the next-best option is to buy a thin plastic tablecloth.

10 Vise Blocks Add Bite

One of the biggest complaints woodworkers have with their vise is that it doesn't hold the work very well when they clamp using only one side of the jaw. The jaw bends a little bit – especially with wooden vises – and this weakens its grip on the work.

The solution is so simple I'm surprised that I don't see this more often. Put a block of equal thickness on the other side of the jaw and your problem is solved. I have a set of "vise blocks" in the most common thicknesses I deal with (½", ⅝", ¾", ⅞" and 1"). To help me out even more, I drive a ¾" dowel through each block to prevent it from dropping when I release the vise. This quick and simple fix will save you a lot of future frustration.

Vise block

Dowel

Vise blocks improve the holding power of any vise. The dowel prevents the block from dropping to the floor when you open the vise.

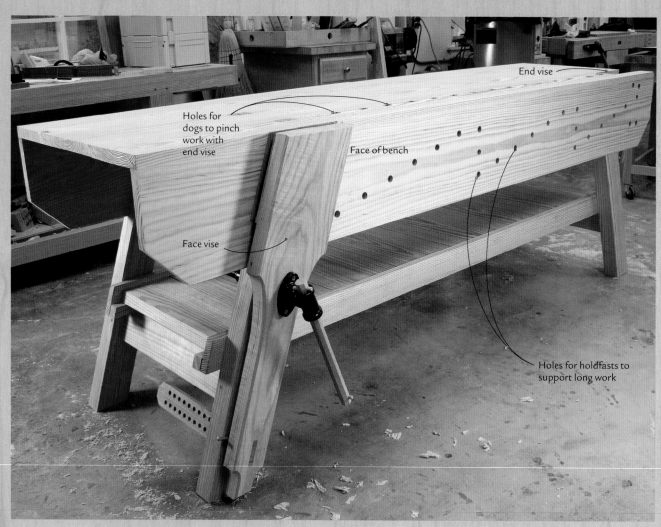

Holes for
dogs to pinch
work with
end vise

End vise

Face of bench

Face vise

Holes for holdfasts to
support long work

This workbench form is uncommon today, but it is still a sound bench
because it allows you to perform all of the critical workbench operations with relative ease. Benches are a triumph of function over form.

This rig serves as the assembly bench in the
Popular Woodworking shop, but if you put
a vise on it somewhere, it probably could
serve as a workbench in a production
shop. It is simple and allows great flexibility for clamping. But some basic operations with this setup would be tricky.

Rules for Workbenches

by Christopher Schwarz

When it comes to building or buying a bench, most woodworkers get wrapped up in what form it should take. Should it be a continental bench popularized by Frank Klausz? A Shaker bench like the one at the Hancock community? How about a British version like Ian Kirby's?

Copying a well-known form is a natural tack to take. After all, when woodworkers buy or build their first workbench, they are in the early stages of learning the craft. They don't know what sort of bench or vises they need, or why one bench looks different than another. So they pick a form that looks good to them – occasionally mixing and matching bits and pieces from different forms – and get busy.

That, I believe, is the seed of the problem with workbenches today. Many commercial workbenches are missing key functions that make work-holding easier. And many classic bench forms get built with modifications that make them frustrating in use.

What's worse, the user might not even know that he or she is struggling. Woodworking is a solitary pursuit, and it's rare to use someone else's bench.

During the last 10 years, I've built a number of classic bench forms, and I've worked on craftsman-made and commercial benches of different stripes. I've been stunned by how awful some workbenches can be at some tasks, and I've also seen brilliantly realized designs.

And now, after all this work, I've concluded that it doesn't matter what sort of bench you have as long as it performs a set of core functions with ease. I've boiled down these core functions into 10 rules for building (or buying) a workbench. As long as your bench obeys these rules (or most of them), you will be able to hold almost any workpiece for any task with a minimum of fuss. This will add speed and enjoyment to your time in the shop and reduce the amount of time you fuss with setups.

Do You Even Need a Bench?

Before we get to the rules, it's fair to say that a lot of the best commercial woodworking today is done on benches that disregard many of these rules. In production shops, it's rare to find a traditional bench used in a traditional manner. More often, a commercial woodworker will have something akin to a clamping table, or even a door on sawhorses. And they can turn out high-quality work that will blow you away.

In 2006 I was teaching a class in hand work at a school where Thomas Stangeland, a maestro at Greene & Greene-inspired work, was also teaching a class. Though we both strive for the same result in craftsmanship, the processes we use couldn't be more different. He builds furniture for a living, and he enjoys it. I build furniture because I enjoy it, and I sell an occasional piece.

One evening we each gave a presentation to the students about our work and I showed an image of the enormous French workbench I'd built the year before and discussed its unusual history.

Thomas then got up and said he wished he had a picture of his workbench: a door on a couple horses. He said that a commercial shop had no time to waste on building a traditional bench. And with his power-tool approach, all he needs is a flat surface.

It's hard to argue with the end result. His furniture is beautiful.

But what's important here is that while you can build with the door-off-the-floor approach, there are many commercial woodworkers who still see the utility of a traditional workbench. Chairmaker and furniture maker Brian Boggs uses more newfangled routers and shop-made devices with aluminum extrusions than I have ever seen. And he still has two enormous traditional workbenches that see constant use. Before Kelly Mehler opened a woodworking school, I visited his commercial shop and got a chance to inspect his vintage bench, which saw daily use.

The point is that a good bench won't make you a better woodworker, and a not-quite-a-bench won't doom you to failure. But a

This French-style workbench weighs more than 325 pounds. The top is 4" thick. The legs are 5" square. All this mass absorbs vibration and makes every cutting operation smoother.

good bench will make many operations easier. It's simply a tool: the biggest clamp in the shop.

Rule No. 1: Always Add Mass

Always overbuild your workbench by adding mass. There is a saying in boatbuilding: If it looks fair, it is fair. For workbenches, here's a maxim: If it looks stout, then make it doubly so. Everything about a workbench takes punishment that is akin to a kitchen chair in a house full of 8-year-old boys.

Early Roman workbenches were built like a Windsor chair. Stout legs were tenoned into a massive top and wedged in place. Traditional French workbenches had massive tops (6" thick), with legs that were big enough to be called tree trunks. Later

Spindly workbenches are nothing new. This anemic example from the early 20th century is too small and lacks mass. Sadly, there are modern ones that are even worse.

workbenches relied more on engineering than mass. The classic continental-style workbench uses a trestle design and dovetails in the aprons and vises to create a bench for the ages. The 19th-century English workbench uses an early torsion-box design to create a stable place to work. And good-quality modern workbenches use threaded rods and bolts to tighten up a design that lacks mass.

Many inexpensive commercial benches are ridiculously rickety. They sway and rack under hand pressure. You can push them across your shop by performing simple operations: routing, sawing, planing. If the bench looks delicate or its components are sized like a modern dining table, I would take a closer look before committing.

A big thick top and stout legs add mass that will help your work. Heavy cabinet saws with lots of cast iron tend to run smoother. The same goes with benches. Once your bench hits about 300 pounds, it won't move unless you want it to move.

Rule No. 2: Use Stout Joints

Overbuild your workbench by using the best joints. These are times to whip out the through-tenon and dovetail.

If you followed rule No. 1, then rule No. 2 should be no problem. Your joints will be sized to fit the massive scale of your components. If you cannot rely on mass, then you should beef things up with superior joinery. While dovetails and through-tenons are overkill for a towel rack, they are good for a bench.

That's because you are applying racking force to the workbench with typical operations and your vises will do their best to tear apart your bench. All wooden vises need to be overbuilt or they will self-destruct when you cinch them down hard. I've even seen a vise rip a benchtop from its base.

Think big when cutting the joints for your workbench. The small tenons are 1¼" thick and 2½" long. The larger tenons are 2½" thick and 2" long.

Make your tenons thick and your mortises deep. If you know how to drawbore a mortise-and-tenon joint, this is one good application. Have you ever been in a timber-framed barn? Did you look at the joints? They're massive and pegged. Imitate that.

I think benches are a good place to practice your skills at cutting these classic joints, but some woodworkers still resist. If that's you, you should investigate hardware to strengthen your bench. Threaded rods, bed bolts, Veritas bench bolts or even stove bolts can turn a spindly assembly into something rigid that can be snugged up if it loosens. The hardware won't give you mass, but it will strengthen a rickety assembly.

Rule No. 3: Pick Your Wood Based on Its Stiffness, Not Its Species

Use a stiff, inexpensive and common wood to build your bench. Showcase benches made from exotic materials are nice. No argument there. But focus on the functions before the flash. I'd rather have a construction-lumber bench that followed all these rules than a beautiful European beech bench that skipped even one of these concepts.

There's a lot of confusion on picking a wood for a bench. Most European benches were built using fine-grained steamed European beech. And many woodworkers go to lengths to purchase precious beech for their workbenches. After all, who wants to argue with hundreds of years of tradition?

I do. European cabinetmakers didn't choose beech because of some magic quality of *Fagus sylvatica*. They chose it because it was dense, stiff, plentiful and inexpensive. In the United States, beech is dense, stiff, hard to find and (sometimes) a bit spendy. You can, of course, use it to build a bench, but you will pay a pretty penny for

the privilege. And it will have no demonstrable advantage over a bench built from a cheaper species.

Other woodworkers, tacking toward the sensible, use hard or soft maple for their benches, rationalizing that it is like the beech of the New World. And indeed, the maples have all the qualities of a good species for a workbench.

Maple is stiff, resists denting and can span long distances without much of a support structure below it. But so can other species. In fact, if you went by the numbers from the wood technologists alone, you'd build your bench from shagbark hickory, despite its difficult nature. Once you look at the characteristics that make a good

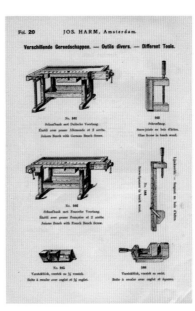

These classic European workbenches were made from fine-grained steamed European beech. Shouldn't you do the same? Not necessarily. Choose a wood that is like beech is in Europe: stiff, inexpensive and plentiful.

species for a workbench, you'll see that white oak, Southern yellow pine, fir or just about any species (excepting basswood and the soft white pines) will perform fine.

Rule No. 4: Use a Tested Design

After you sketch out your workbench design but before you cut any wood, compare your design with historical designs of benches. If your bench appears to be a radical design or looks unlike anything built before, chances are your design is flawed.

I've seen workbenches with pneumatic face vises. Why? I've seen a workbench that had two twin-screw vises: One vise for the right end of the workbench that was matched to work with two long rows of dogs along the length of the benchtop; and a second twin-screw vise on the face of the bench that was matched to two more rows of dogs across the width of the bench.

Now I'm certain that there are a few woodworkers who would really need this arrangement – perhaps someone who has to work on a circular tabletop on one end of the bench and a Windsor chair seat at the other. But for most people who build cabinets and furniture, this setup is redundant and neglects some critical bench functions.

Rule No. 5: The Overall Dimensions of Your Bench Are Critical

Your bench design cannot be too heavy or too long. But its top can easily be too wide or too tall. I think your benchtop should be as long as possible. Find the wall where your workbench will go (hint: Pick the wall that has a window). Measure that space. Subtract four feet from that measurement and that's a good length for the top. Note: The benchtop must be at least 5' long unless you build only small-scale items. Furniture-sized parts typically range up to 48" long and you want to support these fully with a little room to spare.

I've made tops that are 8' long. My next bench will be a 10-footer, the maximum that will fit in my shop. It is difficult to make or imagine a workbench that is too long. The same goes for thickness. It is the thickness that allows the top to be that long. If you make

the top really thick (4" or more), then it will offer unerring support and allow you to build your bench without any support system beneath. The top can perch on the legs and will not sag under its own weight.

The width is a different matter. You can have a bench that is too wide for a one-person shop. I've worked on benches that are 36" wide and they have downsides. For starters, if you park them against the wall you'll have to stretch to reach the tools hanging on the wall. If you assemble projects on your bench, you will find yourself dancing around it a lot more than you should.

But there's more. Cabinetwork is sized in standard chunks. These sizes come from the human body; they aren't arbitrary. A kitchen's base cabinet is generally 24" deep and 34½" high. This is important for a couple reasons. First: It means you don't really need a bench that's much more than 24" deep to build cabinets. With that 24" depth, you actually get some advantages, including the fact that you can clamp the cabinet to your bench from as many as three sides of your bench. That's dang handy. A deep bench allows you to clamp your cabinets to the bench on only two sides (with a couple exceptions). Here's the other thing to keep in mind: Kitchen cabinets are themselves a highly studied work surface. There's a good reason that kitchen cabinets are 24" deep. And it's the same reason you don't want your workbench much deeper either.

Now I'm not going to argue with you if you build really big stuff or have a bench that you share with another woodworker facing you; you might need more depth. But if you are like the rest of us, a 24"-deep bench is a powerful and right-sized tool.

On the issue of workbench height: Many bench builders worry about it and there are a wide variety of rules and advice. The bottom line is the bench must fit you and your work. And in the end, there are no hard-and-fast rules. I wish there were. Some people like low benches; some like them high.

So consider the following as a good place to start. After taking in my crackpot theories, your next stop should be a friend's house or a woodworking supply store to use their benches and get a feel for what is right (it could be as simple as having a bad back that requires you to have a high bench, or a love for wooden handplanes that dictates a low bench).

Here is my experience with bench height: I started with a bench that was 36" high, which seemed right for someone who is 6' 3⅝" tall. And for machine woodworking I was right. The high bench brought the work close to my eyes. I loved it. And then my passion for handwork reared its ugly head.

If you get into hand tools, a high bench becomes less attractive. I started with a jack plane and a few smoothing planes. They worked OK with a high bench, but I became fatigued quickly.

After reading the screed on bench heights, I lowered the height of my 36" bench. It seemed radical, but one day I got the nerve up and sawed 2" off the legs. Those two inches changed my attitude toward planing.

The 34"-bench height allowed me to use my long leg muscles to propel the plane forward instead of my arms.

Now, before you build your next bench at 34" high, stop for a minute. That might not be right for you. Do you use wooden stock planes? If so, you need to consider that the wooden body planes can hold your arms about 3" to 4" higher off the workbench than

Here's proof that odd workbench designs are nothing new. This Hammacher, Schlemmer & Co. bench from an old catalog is a study in tool storage. I've seen one of these in person and I can say this: I would not want to have to build anything using it.

This early 20th-century airplane factory had the right idea when it came to workbench length. With a long bench, you can work on one end and assemble at the other – no need for an assembly bench. Thus, a big bench actually saves floorspace.

a metal plane can. As a result, a wooden plane user's workbench should be lower.

This is as good reason as ever to get to know someone who has a good shop you can visit and discuss your ideas with. It is better not to make this decision on paper alone.

But there are other factors you must consider when settling on the bench's height. How tall are you? If you are over 6' tall, you should scale your bench a bit higher. Start high and cut it down if it's too high. And prop it up on some blocks of wood if it's too low. Experiment. It's not a highboy; it's a workbench.

Here are other things to consider: Do you work with machinery? If so, a bench that's 34" from the floor – or a bit lower – can be good. The top of a table saw is typically 34" from the floor, so a workbench could be (at most) a great outfeed table or (at least) not in the way of your crosscutting and ripping.

Of course, everyone wants a ballpark idea for where to start. So here it is: Stand up straight and drop your arms against your sides in a relaxed manner. Measure from the floor to the place where your pinky joins your hand. That has been the sweet spot for me.

Rule No. 6: Benches Must Hold the Work in Three Ways

All benches should be able to grip the wood so you can easily work on the faces, the ends and the edges. Many commercial benches fail on this point.

Submit your bench to what I call the Kitchen Cabinet Door Test. Imagine a typical kitchen door that is ¾" thick, 15" wide and 23" long. How would you affix that door flat on your bench to level its joints and then sand (or plane) it flat? How would you clamp

Here is how high my workbench is compared to my hand, which is hanging loosely by my side. I use hand and power tools in my work, and I've found this height is ideal.

the door so you could work on the ends to trim the top rail and tops of the stiles so the door will fit its opening? And how will you secure that door on edge so you can rout its hinge mortise and plane off the saw-blade marks without the door flopping around? Does your bench pass this test? OK, now ask the same questions with a door that is ¾" x 15" x 38". And then try a board that is ¾" x 12" x 6'.

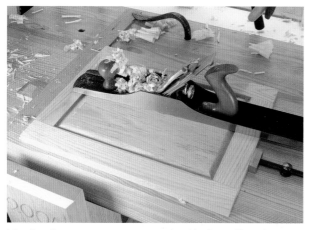

Most benches are easy to set up to work on the faces of boards or assemblies. In this example, a door is clamped between dogs. You can even work simpler and plane against a planing stop.

Working on the ends of boards – especially wide boards – can be a challenge for face vises. Adding a clamp to the setup stabilizes the work for sawing or whatever.

This primitive bench still allows you to work on long edges of boards. The crochet (or hook) grips the board. Holdfasts and a scrap support from below. Simple and brilliant.

How you accomplish each of these three functions is up to you and your taste and budget. To work on the faces of boards, you can use a planing stop, a grippy sanding pad, a tail vise with dogs, clamps or hold-downs.

To work on the ends of boards, you can choose a shoulder vise (especially for dovetailing), a metal quick-release vise, a leg vise or a twin-screw vise. And you can use all of these in conjunction with a clamp across your bench. The vise holds one corner of the work; the clamp holds the other corner.

Working the long edges of boards is tricky with most benches. In fact, most benches make it difficult to work the edges of long boards, doors or face frames. There are a couple ways to solve this. Older benches had the front edge of the benchtop flush with the front of the legs and stretchers so you could clamp your frames and long boards to the legs. And the older benches also would have a sliding deadman (sometimes called a board jack). It would slide back and forth and had an adjustable peg to support the work from below. Another old form of bench, an English design, had a wide front apron that came down from the top that was bored with holes for a peg to support long work.

Rule No. 7: Make Your Bench Friendly to Clamps

Your bench is a three-dimensional clamping surface. Anything that interferes with clamping work to your benchtop (aprons, a drawer bank, doors, supports etc.) can make some operations a challenge.

We had a phase at *Popular Woodworking* where we tried to design a cupholder into every project. It started innocently with a deck chair. Who doesn't want a cool beverage at hand? Then there was the dartboard. What goes better with darts than beer? I think we came to our senses when designing a series of cupholders into a Gustav Stickley Morris chair reproduction. Do you really need a Big Gulp-sized hole in your Morris chair? I didn't think so.

The point of this story is to illustrate a trend in workbench design that I personally find troubling. It's a knee-jerk reaction to a common American complaint: We don't think we have enough space in our shops to store our tools and accessories. And how do we solve this problem with our workbenches? By designing them like kitchen cabinets with a countertop work surface.

This design approach gives us lots of drawers below the benchtop, which is great for storing the things you reach for every day. It also can make your bench a pain in the hiney to use for many common operations, such as clamping things to your bench.

Filling up the space below the benchtop also prohibits you from using any type of holdfast or holddown that I'm aware of.

If you build drawers below the top, how will you clamp objects to the benchtop to work with them? Typically, the banks of drawers below the benchtop prohibit a typical F-style clamp from sneaking in there and lending a hand with the setup. So you can't use a typical clamp to affix a router template to the bench. There are ways around these problems (a tail vise comes to mind) but the tail vise can be a challenge to install, set and use.

You can try to cheat (as I have) and install the drawer bank so there is a substantial space underneath the benchtop for holdfasts and clamps. Or you can give your bench a large overhang to allow clamping (as some Shaker-style workbenches did) but then you have to start engineering a way to hold long boards and assemblies on edge.

Rule No. 8: There are Good Rules for Placing the Vises on Your Bench

Place your vises so they work with your tools. Vises confuse many workbench builders. They're bewildering if you've never spent much time working at a bench to develop a taste for the peccadilloes of all the idiosyncratic forms. There are a lot of weird configurations in the world, from a table with no vises to the bench with a vise on every corner.

Classic workbenches have some sort of vise at the front left corner of the bench. This is called the face vise. Why is it at the left? When we work with hand tools, especially planes, right-handers work from right to left. So having the vise at the left end of the bench is handy because you will always be planing into the vise that is gripping your work, and the work can be braced against the screws of the vise. So if you are a lefty, placing your vise on the front right corner makes sense.

So with that left corner occupied by a vise, where are you going to put the second vise that is designed to grip boards so you can work on their faces? (The classic vise for this is a tail vise.) Well the right side of the bench is free (for right-handers) and there is no disadvantage to placing it there, so that's where it generally goes.

Messing with this arrangement can be trouble. I've seen face vises on the right corner of the bench of people who are right-handed. They said they liked it better for crosscutting with a handsaw. But when and if you start handplaning, that vise will be in the way because it won't be ideal for gripping long stock. It will be holding the tail end of the board and the plane will be trying to pull it out of the vise.

Rule No. 9: No Fancy Finishes

When finishing a workbench, less is more. A shiny film finish allows your work to scoot all over the bench. And a film finish will crack when struck by a hammer or dead-blow mallet. Choose a finish that is easy to apply, offers some protection and doesn't build up a thick film. I like an oil/varnish blend (sold as Danish Oil), or just boiled linseed oil.

Rule No. 10: Get a Window Seat

Try to place your bench against a wall and under a window, especially if you use hand tools. The wall braces the workbench as you are planing cross-grain and sawing. The light from the window points out the flaws in the work that your hand tools are trying to remove. (When I work with hand tools, I turn the overhead lights off. I can see much better with fewer light sources.)

For machine work, I find that placing the bench by a window helps with some operations, though not all. When power sanding, for example, the raking window light points out scratches better than overhead lighting.

In general, when working with power tools, I tend to pull my workbench away from the wall so I can work on all sides of it. When working with routers, you sometimes have to work with odd clamping setups so that you can rout around a template. So having access to all four sides of the bench is handy. Power tool

An oil-varnish blend (any brand) is an ideal finish for a workbench. It resists stains, doesn't build up a film and is easy to apply. Two coats are all I ever use.

Here's another historical bench that shows some difficulties. The drawers will interfere with clamping things down to the bench. With no dogs or tail vise, this bench could be frustrating to work on.

setups thrive on overhead light — and lots of it. So being by the window is nice, but not as necessary.

How to Fix Your Current Bench

You don't have to build or buy a new workbench if you're frustrated with the one you have. There are ways to improve your bench so it will be more useful. Here are some strategies.

Problem No. 1: My bench is too lightweight. I chase it around the shop when working.

 Add weight by building a tray below the bench and fill it with sand. Or rebuild your bench base with massive components and joints. You also can build drawers near the floor (so they don't impede clamping things to the top). That adds weight and storage.

Problem No. 2: My bench sways and vibrates when I work, making my saw cuts and attempts at planing into a ragged mess.

Your problem is most likely in the base of the bench. Commercial benches can be too spindly for woodworking. Rebuild the base from massive components and better joints. If you can't do that, stiffen the bench by running all-thread rod through the legs and cinching the base tight with nuts.

Problem No. 3: I want a new bench, but I'm low on funds.

Build your bench using Southern yellow pine or fir, both of which are stiff, plentiful and cheap (you can build a bench for less than $250, easy). You will have to pick your lumber with care and let it reach equilibrium with your shop. But in the end, you'll have a great bench.

Problem No. 4: I think I want a fancy twin-screw vise, Emmert patternmaker's vise or tail vise on my bench. Plus something for working metal.

Before you drop serious coin on vises and put them on every corner, start with a simple face vise. Then buy a tail vise. Then decide after a year of working on the bench if you need the fancier vises. The answer might be yes. You also might forget that you ever wanted those vises.

Problem No. 5: My bench is too short, too wide, narrow, high or low.

If your bench is too short you should probably build a new top. Keep the base if you can. If it's too wide, rip it down (removing a tool tray will help). You might need to cut the base a bit narrower as well. This is doable: Cut the stretchers on the sides shorter and

You do need to be able to pull your bench away from the wall on occasion. When I am assembling cabinets, I'll clamp them to the benchtop so I'm able to get around the bench. The same goes when I'm routing. Note how I'm harnessing the window light.

With your workbench against the wall, you have the wall and the mass of your bench holding things steady as you saw your workpieces. You also can keep your tools at arm's length. And, the windows cast a useful light on your workbench.

then cut tenons on their ends. Cut new mortises on the legs and assemble it. If your bench is too narrow, scab on new material at the back, which will add mass as well. If your bench is too high, cut down the legs or the sled foot. If it's too low, build a sled foot to raise it.

Problem No. 6: My bench makes it difficult to work on the long edges of boards.

First, detach the benchtop from its base and reattach it so the legs are flush with the front edge of the benchtop. If your bench has a sled foot or a trestle design, there is an easier fix. Scab on extra pieces to the legs to bring them flush with the front of the benchtop. Now build a sliding deadman or a bench slave and you'll be in business.

Problem No. 7: My bench looks like a kitchen counter with drawers below. Clamping to the bench is a problem.

You might be stuck here. Some commercial designs allow you to remove the drawer bank (they sell them separately) and you can install it someplace else handy, such as under a table saw's wing. If your bench is a door on top of base cabinets, consider making a new base and use that cabinet as a cabinet.

Problem No. 8: My commercial bench came with a face vise and tail vise. Both rack horribly. How do I improve them?

By throwing them in the fireplace and installing a real face vise on the front and tail vise on the end.

Problem No. 9: My workbench has a lacquer finish that looks nasty and lets the work slide everywhere.

Flatten the top of your workbench and then refinish the top with an oil/varnish blend.

Problem No. 10: I like my bench in the middle of the room so I can work on all sides.

Perhaps you do. Try putting it under a window and against the wall and work that way for a few months. Don't have a window? Directional lighting fixtures can help. Or you can save your pennies and have a window installed. I did. It was the best $1,000 I've ever spent on my shop.

Most workbench books begin with a grand statement about how the workbench is the most useful tool in the shop. I'm not so sure I agree with that statement as it stands. I think it's correct to say that a well-designed, solidly built and properly outfitted bench is the most useful tool in the workshop. Anything less is only making you struggle.

Workbench Gallery

There is a lot to take into consideration when you go about choosing a workbench design for your shop. Depending on what you build and what methods you use you'll have different workholding requirements. You may also find that you'd like to have a bench that allows for storage as well as workholding. Your choice of bench design is a personal one and you should approach it thoughtfully and research all the possibilities. This gallery gives you a peak at a few different workbench designs with different attributes that may or may not suit your needs. For additional insight into getting the most functionality out of your workbench the following two resources may be helpful: "Workbenches from Design & Theory to Construction & Use" and "The Workbench Design Book," both by Christopher Schwarz.

The Holtzapffel workbench has old-world features, such as its tree-trunk legs. And it has elaborate workholding, such as its sexy-looking tail vise. Unlike some other benches of this era, the Holtzapffel blends several traditions to create an effective bench. This 19th-century workbench can be built with bolts to be knocked down, or it can be built as a permanent addition to your shop as shown here.

This English bench is based on a bench from Peter Nicholson's "Mechanic's Companion." And thought the design is old, what's under those aprons is considered quite modern: a torsion box. The wide front apron, angled legs and jack-legged vise are all unfamiliar to most modern woodworkers. However, about 200 years ago, each of these features could be found on benches for carpenters and joiners. These features disappeared as the continental bench became the preferred form.

Want a workbench that allows for tons of storage? This Shaker workbench design features generous amounts of space for working with your tools and for storing them when you are done.

The allure of an 18th-century French workbench comes from its sliding dovetail through-joints and its massive parts. The only thing more stout would be a bench carved from solid rock. This bench will not rack or move as you work. Plus, the heft of this bench allows it to absorb vibration allowing for smooth cutting operations.

This modern bench combines features from several historic forms from the Roubo to the Workmate. With tool trays in the center and a shelf below there is ample room for both storage and work space.

For those who prefer power tools, this bench gives you a smaller traditional bench for your hand work along with a cavernous place for hand tools and hand-held power tool storage in the drawers and on the large shelf underneath the top.

You don't have to spend a fortune to build a great bench. This bench uses southern yellow pine from a box store to keep the cost low. You could also use fir or poplar.

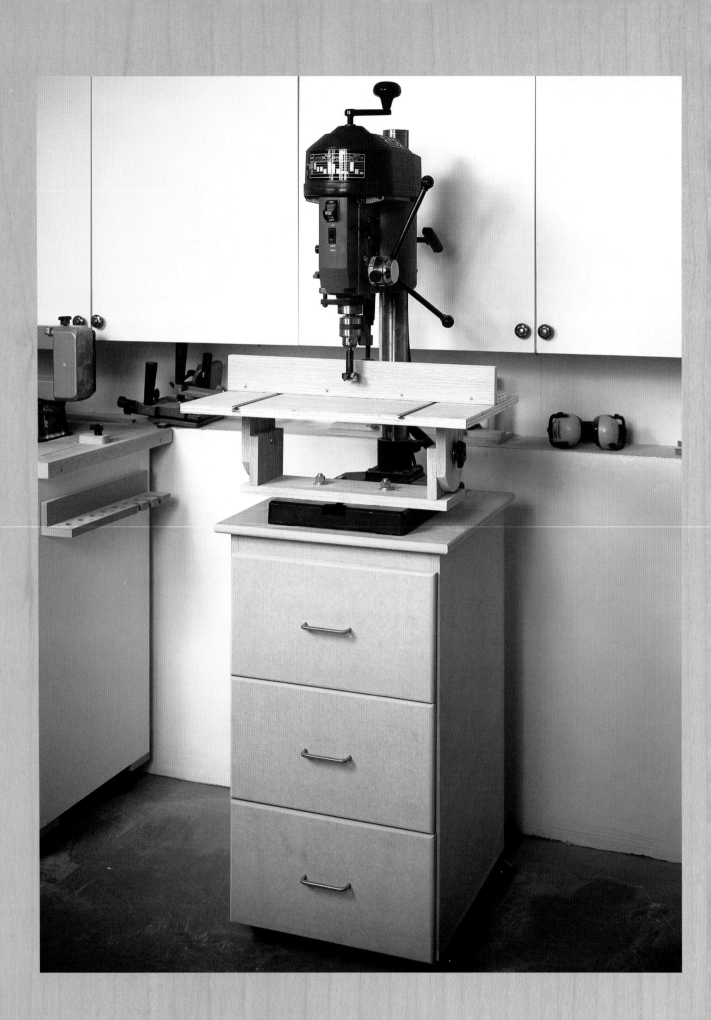

Chapter Eleven

Placing Machinery

by Scott Gibson

In a much earlier era, cabinetmakers didn't spend much time worrying about where to put machines in their shops. They didn't have much to work with. A small shop might have had a communal lathe turned by an apprentice, but artisans worked mostly at their benches with hand tools. Period drawings of these old shops make it clear just how far we've come.

Anyone setting up shop these days can choose from a tremendous variety of stationary and portable power tools. Manufacturers from Pacific Rim countries, from the United States and from Europe, all competing in a world market, have helped to keep tool prices stable. New designs are safer and more innovative. It's good news for someone just getting interested in the craft.

Finding the right spot to set up shop, covered in Chapter 1 of this section, has a way of helping us decide which tools are most important. Small spaces dictate a very careful selection of essential tools. A larger space invites more freedom. But either way, figuring out exactly where to put those tools is an essential next step.

No two woodworkers are likely to agree on how a shop should be organized. The "best" arrangement depends on a variety of factors — what's being produced, for example, as well as individual work habits. That said, no matter what the shop, machinery should be arranged to eliminate extra steps and extra work while leaving enough elbow room for both safety and comfort.

Machinery Essentials for a Small Shop

Woodworking can cover anything from turning wooden pen bodies to building an armoire or a Windsor chair. What we make will help shape the list of machine tools we invest in and how we organize them in the shop.

At one end of the spectrum are woodworkers such as Alan Bradstreet, a Maine professional who turns out a single product — bookmarks made from thin strips of cherry. Every machine in his shop is part of a well-organized progression that transforms blocks of scrap cherry into finished bookmarks. Every tool is devoted to this end, and all of them are precisely placed for efficiency.

Chairmaker Brian Boggs's former Kentucky based shop is a good example of a shop for a woodworker with specialized needs (see photos on page 76).

Most of us, however, are woodworking generalists who might make a dining table one month and a wall cabinet or chair the next.

The basic stationary tools for this kind of woodworking are a table saw, a jointer and a planer. These three tools allow you to turn rough lumber into finished goods, and you really need all three of them. A typical setup for a small shop would include a 10" table saw, a jointer with a minimum capacity of 6" and a 12" thickness planer.

There are woodworkers who would swap a band saw for a table saw (for one thing, band saws are safer). But even in these shops the

Norm Abram's New Yankee Workshop housed a number of dedicated woodworking machines. The ample floor plan allows this approach, but smaller shops may consider combination machines to save space.

The type of work produced in a shop dictates the size and variety of woodworking machinery. Chairmaker Brian Boggs doesn't need a table saw, which is a mainstay in most cabinet shops. For him, a band saw and specialized joint-cutting equipment are more useful.

This shop allows plenty of infeed and outfeed room for the table saw. Tom Willenborg incorporated a second table saw in the extension table of his cabinet saw for a dado stack that's always ready to go.

basic steps remain the same: Rough lumber must be flattened (face jointed) and straightened on a jointer, then run through a planer to a uniform thickness and finally cut to length and width on a saw. Only then can you make something out of it.

Many woodworkers start with these basics and build on them in time by adding a drill press, stationary belt sander or disc sander, mortising machine, shaper and spindle sander.

Dedicated Tools or Combination Machines?

If the table saw/jointer/planer combination is to be the tool foundation of most new shops, there's still the question of whether to buy three separate machines or a combination machine that will handle two or more basic functions. There are good arguments for and against each solution.

Dedicated machines are always ready to go – they don't have to be converted from one thing to another – and that saves both time and effort. Separate machines obviously take up more room, but they also can be less expensive and there are more brands from which to choose. There's a brisk market in used tools, so it should be possible to get started on even a fairly modest budget.

Combination machines have some advantages, too. Primarily, of course, they save space. In a very small workshop, a combination planer/jointer eliminates one bulky piece of equipment. And because these tools use a common set of knives for jointing and thickness planing, you'll be able to flatten wide pieces of lumber. That's a very big advantage. The Robland X310, for example, which combines a total of five machines in one, comes with 12" knives for jointing and planing.

The downside to combination machines is that it takes time to switch from one function to another. Key settings – such as the position of the fence – might have to be changed in switching from one job to another. Combination machines also tend to be more expensive than separate machines that do the same jobs. Even with these drawbacks, they're worth considering for very small shops.

Finding a Layout that Works in Your Space

If you've never set up a shop before, it's going to be hard to visualize the many possible layouts in the space you have to work with. Machines are not only heavy, but they frequently require special connections – a 220/240-volt receptacle, for example, or a connection to the dust collection system. With that in mind, it makes sense to do as much as you can on paper before pushing machines around the shop.

Start by drawing a floor plan of the shop exactly to scale. Mark on it the locations of windows, doors, electrical outlets and any other features that might affect the operation of a stationary tool. Now make cutouts, also to scale, of each machine you need to find a home for. It's easy to move the machines around on paper.

Each machine requires a certain amount of clearance between it and nearby objects. Think of it as the tool's aura. For example, a table saw must be positioned so that long pieces of lumber can be run over the blade and ripped. Eight feet is a minimum benchmark for solid lumber (that's also the length of a full-size piece of plywood), so you'll need a space that's longer than 16' in which to place the table saw. It's better to allow a few extra feet on each end. You'll also need space on the left side of the saw so you can maneuver a full sheet of plywood up on the table.

A jointer and planer also need generous allowances of room on both the infeed and outfeed sides. But because you are more likely to cut stock roughly to length before jointing and planing, you may not need quite as much room as you would with the table saw. And you won't need nearly as much width.

In a large shop it won't be a problem locating the saw to provide these kinds of clearances. In a small shop, you may need to take advantage of a window or a door. You might, for example, give yourself 12' of space on the infeed side of the table saw and only 6' on the outfeed side. By positioning the saw near a door, you can always accommodate those extra-length boards when you need to.

Another key element is the relative heights of adjacent tools and fixtures. You might, for example, have plenty of room on infeed and outfeed sides of a table saw to handle long pieces of stock. That part of it works out just fine. But what about potential interference on the side? Maybe you were planning on putting a workbench several feet to the left of the table saw. If it's just an inch or two higher than the saw, the distance between the two becomes the maximum length of stock you can crosscut.

If you weigh these relationships in advance they often can be solved without much trouble. In the case of a nearby bench, raising the saw slightly on blocks or cutting down the legs of the bench a bit may fix the problem.

Taking this idea one step further, consider building simple models of your shop and tools out of cardboard or foam board. Make them to scale and move things around until you're satisfied you've got a plan. It takes more time than working on paper, but you'll get a three-dimensional look at what your shop will look and feel like.

Think About Work Flow

You'll probably end up buying rough lumber in lengths much longer than what you'll eventually need. You may be building a wall cabinet that's only 3' high, but the rough lumber could easily be 12' or more in length when you get it home. So one of the first steps is to place tools so that you can break the raw material into manageable pieces.

Close to the entry along one side of the shop is a good place to put a long bench, as well as a centrally located chop saw and nearby storage racks for both lumber and plywood. A long board can be cut to rough length before it travels around the shop.

Locating the storage bin for sheet goods close to the table saw makes it easier to cut pieces of plywood or particleboard to size. Sheet goods tend to be quite heavy – a 4' x 8' sheet of Medium-Density Fiberboard (MDF) ¾" thick can weigh close to 100 pounds – so it doesn't make sense carrying them any farther than necessary.

What comes next? Usually, the lumber will need to be flattened and straightened on the jointer and then sent through the thickness planer. Locating these two machines (or combination machine) nearby and close to the table saw will save some steps.

A power miter saw centered on a bench against a wall can cut long pieces of stock into more manageable pieces. By locating the saw near the entry door and storage racks, you won't have to maneuver long pieces of wood through the shop.

These machines can be located very close to one another as long as the stock doesn't bump into anything else while it's being processed. For example, you might group the table saw, jointer and planer in line in the middle of a small shop so that stock runs from side to side, the full width of the space.

A Working Triangle for the Woodshop

This idea of grouping machines for efficiency and comfort is the same as creating a work triangle in the kitchen. In a kitchen, this is the relationship between the sink, stove and refrigerator. In a shop it might be the relationship between machines that are used most frequently.

Suppose, for example, you expect to resaw stock for bookmatched panels on a fairly regular basis. The process involves a band saw (to slice the full width of a board) as well as frequent trips to a jointer so the cut side of the board can be trued up. In a shop like this, the work triangle might include band saw, jointer and possibly a miter saw or table saw.

The work triangle in kitchen design is a relatively rigid planning guide. Some designers go so far as to prescribe minimum and maximum distances when you add up all three legs of the triangle. English kitchen designer Johnny Grey favors a much more flexible approach that can be applied to a workshop as well as a kitchen.

Grey starts by accounting for all the important workstations in a kitchen. That includes the sink, food preparation areas, stove, refrigerator and so forth – roughly a dozen in all. Then he thinks of the paths people will travel to get from one function to another. These are not necessarily straight lines that can't be bent. Instead, he thinks of them as rubber bands that have some flexibility but can't be completely severed.

In a workshop, as in a kitchen, no floor plan will perfectly accommodate everything we do. The idea is to think about operations we commonly undertake and design around them. As long as movement around the shop and between machines is unobstructed and logical, the machine layout will probably work most of the time.

Some Machines Don't Need Much Space

It's easy to think of machine placement only in terms of the bigger pieces of equipment. That makes sense because they are the hardest to place and tend to dominate the work environment. But there are many smaller machines that can be worked in around the edges of a shop. They may not need as much room around them because the workpieces we usually bring to them are much smaller.

A bench grinder doesn't take up very much space and can easily be tucked in a corner because the workpieces are short – you sure don't need much clearance for a chisel or plane iron. The same is true of a drill press and a horizontal boring machine. They seldom require the kind of clearances that a table saw, jointer or planer must have.

Smaller tools can sometimes share space. A hollow-chisel mortising machine doesn't have a very large footprint but you occasionally may want to cut mortises in fairly long pieces of stock. Housing the tool on the same long bench as a miter saw is one way of dealing with it.

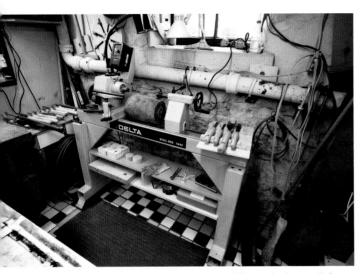

This lathe is pushed right up against the wall to make the most of a small basement workshop. Some tools don't require much space around them, making them good candidates for overlooked corners and nooks.

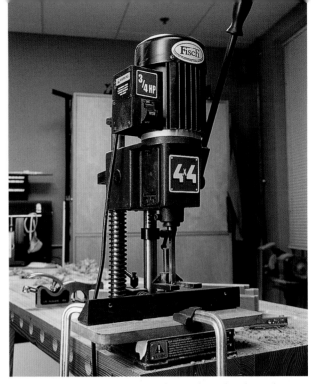

When space is at a premium, tuck infrequently used tools in cabinets, under workbenches or otherwise out of the way until they're needed. They can be mounted temporarily in just a few minutes.

In finding homes for small pieces of equipment, a key consideration is how often they are used. That grinder, for example, may be only an occasional tool for many woodworkers, something we use once a month to regrind edge chisels or plane blades. In that case, it can be housed in a distant corner of the shop, preferably near good natural light, or even mounted to a board that can be put in a storage cabinet when it's not needed.

If, on the other hand, you're going to do a lot of turning, you may need to make frequent trips to the grinder to touch up your tools. You'd probably want the grinder right next to the lathe or just a few steps away.

Don't overlook out-of-the-way nooks and crannies when trying to shoehorn in all your tools in a shop. There's no reason a compressor has to take up floor space in a small shop when it could just as easily be stored beneath a bench. You may not need a separate router table if you use part of your table saw's extension table for that purpose. In a small shop, consolidate where you can and give up dedicated floor space only to those tools that are used all the time.

Mobile Tools Can Make Small Spaces Serve Many Needs

When the woodshop takes over the garage, the car often winds up outside. But by making some machines mobile, even a single-car garage can accommodate both needs.

Scott Landis, in "The Workshop Book" (Taunton Press), visits one woodworker who has made this arrangement work and no doubt there are countless others. Maurice Gordon, who had only 420 square feet to work with, used a computer-design program to plan his shop. It houses a full complement of tools – everything from a table saw to a scroll saw, and lumber storage to boot. But when it's time to put the car away, the planer, table saw, band saw, jointer and sander can be rolled out of the way.

Gordon's shop is a marvel of good planning and it revolves around good-quality mobile bases for large stationary power

tools. Even a full-sized cabinet saw with an extended table can be mounted on a mobile base. When the wheels are retracted, the saw is rock-solid. When it needs to be moved, one person can push it across the floor.

Even if you don't need to make room for the family sedan, mounting some tools on wheels is a great way to create more elbow room in a small shop. Consider a wheeled base for a planer, for instance, which you'll probably use less often than a table saw.

You might want to invest in bases for heavy stationary tools, but a variety of other shop fixtures and tools can be put on bases of your own making. When looking for casters, invest in models where both wheels and spindles can be locked. Casters with wheel-only locking mechanisms are cheaper but you may find the tool has an annoying habit of moving around while you try to use it.

Be Ready to Try New Ideas

Even with careful planning, it's tough to get everything in exactly the right spot your first time out. Many woodworkers will continue to tinker with shop layout and machinery locations for as long as they inhabit the space.

The kind of shop you have certainly affects how much flexibility you have to alter machine placements. If you're building a new shop from scratch and plan to start with a concrete slab, you can cast electrical conduit in the floor to get power to exactly where it's needed. That's a big plus, but it also calls for very careful planning and won't allow much tinkering later.

But for those at work in shops with more forgiving floors, experimentation with shop layout is going to be a plus.

Adding a new tool to an existing inventory may require some juggling of equipment. You might borrow an idea from another workshop. Whatever the reason for changes, tool placement is one of those things that's never really cast in stone.

The cabinets in this organized shop have sliding storage shelves for easy access to tools that aren't used every day.

Space beneath the long extension table on this full-sized cabinet saw is too valuable to waste. This storage cabinet holds saw blades, a dado set and other table saw accessories.

Even in a very large shop, there's no reason to give up floor space to tools that can work just as effectively under a bench or in an outdoor storage area. Air compressors and dust collectors are two candidates for this treatment.

Making a tool mobile is an excellent way of making your shop more flexible. Putting a miter saw or a drill press on a custom stand that includes its own storage allows these tools to be pushed out of the way when they are not needed.

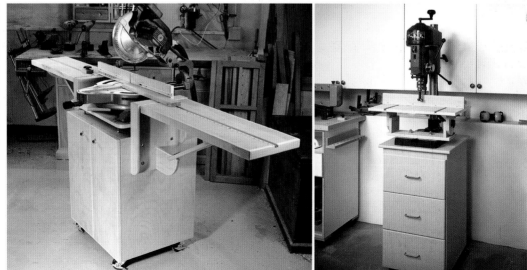

Chapter Twelve

One-Weekend Router Table

by David Thiel

I think it might have been seeing a $1,000 router table setup at a recent woodworking show (it's very cool, but $1,000?). Or maybe it was realizing that our shop's router table's cabinet mostly takes up space and fills with dust. Either of these observations was enough to get us rethinking our router table needs.

Essentially you need a stable, flat working surface that can support most work. You need a fence that guides, supports and moves easily for adjustments (both the fence location on the table and the faces themselves toward the bit). You also need easy access to the router for bit changing and height adjustment. Other than that, it just needs to be up off the floor, hence the cabinet.

So we decided that a lightweight, easily stored router tabletop that would still offer all these benefits would be preferable. Oh, and we wanted to be able to make it in a weekend for less than $120. No problem! The hardware came to $65 and change. You should be able to purchase the plywood for around $50.

Allowing the proper clearance for your router is critical. You can see that I've removed the handles from the tool to allow as much space as possible. Mark out the space and then assemble the frame to fit.

An Ingenious Design

For a stable, lightweight top the solution that made sense was a torsion box made of high-density plywood. The size that seemed most functional was a 20"-deep x 24"-wide platform that only needed to be about 4" tall. The box itself has an open center section on the bottom to accommodate the router body. There are two lengths of T-track installed front to back on the tabletop to easily reposition the fence.

The fence itself is a variation of one we've built half-a-dozen times. The fence base is almost a torsion box — more of a torsion corner — that provides stable support for the laterally adjustable fence faces and allows for dust hook-up.

For the router itself, we went shopping. After looking at a number of router lifts and router table plates we chose the Milwaukee 5625-29, a 3½ horsepower router that offers through-the-base height adjustment. And, no, the price of the router is not included in the $120 figure. You don't have to use this router, but in our opinion it has the horsepower you want to swing large panel-raising bits on your router table, and the through-the-base adjustment means you don't need to buy a router lift. The variable speed is also a big plus.

We chose a circular router plate from Veritas because it replaces the sole plate on your router and allows you to still use the router freehand or in the table without changing the base. The base also fits into the table without the use of any tools, and slips in and out from above in seconds.

Now the fun part: To bring the router table up to height, but still make it compact, we designed a brace that is mounted to the table and then the entire thing is simply clamped in your bench vise. Instant router table!

Torsion Top Construction

The top itself is very simple to make. A frame made of ¾" x 3" plywood pieces is sandwiched between two pieces of ¾" plywood. The bottom piece is notched to accommodate your router (you'll need to test fit your router to locate the center frame pieces and the notch). The top piece extends 1½" beyond the frame on all sides to allow for clamping featherboards or other guides to the top surface.

Start by cutting out the top, bottom and seven frame pieces. If you opt to use the Veritas plate, the instructions are very clear on how to cut the hole in the tabletop to fit the plate. Otherwise, follow the instructions for your individual router plate.

We chose to locate the router plate closer to the front of the table rather than in the center of the table. Most router table work happens within 6" of the fence and this location keeps you from having to lean across the table for operations. If you have a larger piece to run, the fence can be reversed on the table to give you a larger support surface.

With the router plate located in the top, suspend the router from the top and locate the two center frame members the necessary distance to clear the router. Make a note of that dimension, then lay out your frame accordingly.

I used glue and an 18-gauge brad nailer to assemble all the pieces for this project. While perhaps not the height of joinery, it's fast and reliable.

With the frame assembled, place the frame on the bottom, and mark and notch the center section to allow clearance space for the router body. You could leave the center section open, but the extra strength along the back of the tabletop is worth the effort.

Attach the bottom the same way you assembled the frame.

Before fastening the top to the table, you need to install the aluminum T-track inserts for fence adjustment. I used a dado set on my table saw to run the grooves before attaching the top.

Next, attach the top, centering it on the frame assembly. Pay extra attention when attaching the top to keep the fasteners below the surface of the tabletop. This will keep you from scratching your

More marking: With the frame assembled and resting on the bottom piece, mark out the notch that will allow the router to extend through the top.

With the bottom notched, simply glue and nail it in place on the frame.

One-weekend Router Table

NO.	LET.	ITEM	DIMENSIONS (INCHES)			MATERIAL
			T	W	L	
1	T1	Top	¾	20	24	Plywood
1	B1	Bottom	¾	17	21	Plywood
2	B2	Frame F&B	¾	3	21	Plywood
4	B3	Frame dividers	¾	3	15½	Plywood
1	B4	Frame divider	¾	3	10½	Plywood
2	B5	Support stems	¾	3	7	Plywood
2	B6	Support braces	¾	3	21	Plywood
2	F1	Fence faces	¾	4	14	Plywood
1	F2	Fence sub-face	½	3½	28	Plywood
1	F3	Fence base	½	3	28	Plywood
4	F4	Fence braces	¾	3	3	Plywood
1	F5	Hood top	½	5	3½	Plywood
2	F6	Hood sides	½	2½	3	Plywood
1	F7	Hood back	½	5	3	Plywood
2	H1	Fence T-tracks	⅜	¾	14	Aluminum
4	H2	Hex-head bolts	¼	20	1½	
4	H3	Star knobs				
2	H4	Cam clamps				
2	H5	Table T-tracks	⅜	¾	20	Aluminum

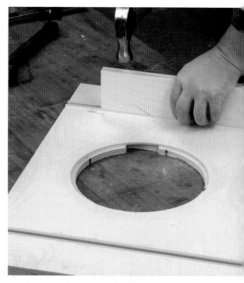

After cutting the grooves for the T-track, tap it in place using a backing block. If you have to tap too hard with the hammer, your groove is too small. Attach the track with ½" x #4 flathead screws. Pre-drill and countersink each hole.

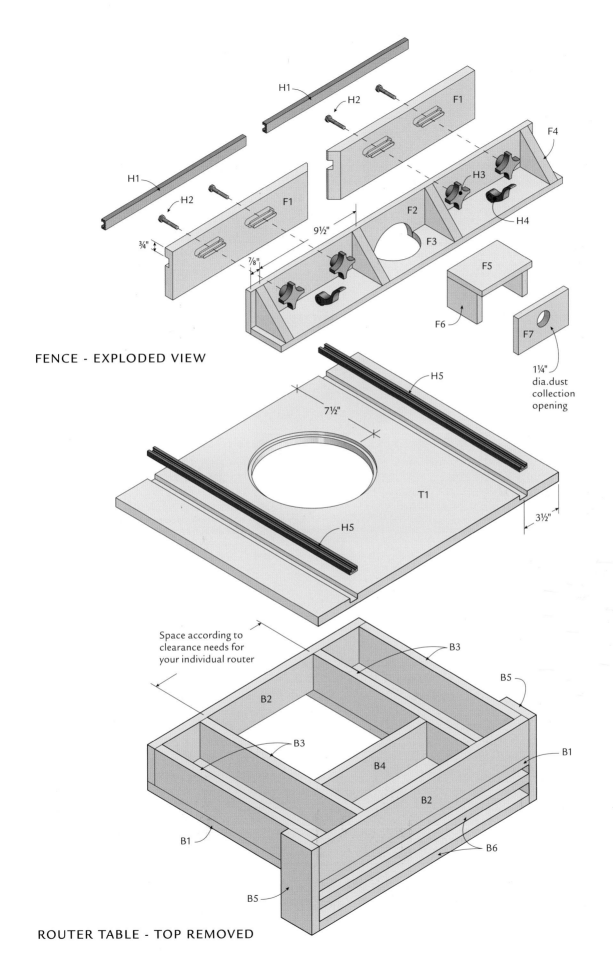

H1

H2

F1

F4

H1

H2

H3

F1

H4

9½"

F2

F3

¾"

F5

⅞"

F6

F7

1¼" dia.dust collection opening

FENCE - EXPLODED VIEW

H5

7½"

T1

3½"

H5

Space according to clearance needs for your individual router

B3

B2

B5

B3

B4

B1

B2

B1

B2

B6

B5

ROUTER TABLE - TOP REMOVED

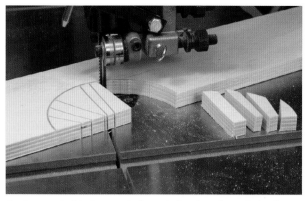

Cutting out the bit clearance hole on the band saw is made simple by first cutting "spokes" toward your line. These relief cuts allow the pieces to fall out in small chunks, rather than fighting with one bigger piece.

With the sub-face and base assembled, add the four triangular braces with glue and brads. Space them adequately to support the fence, but make sure you leave room for the knobs.

The dust collection hood completes the router table fence. It should seal tightly around the fence to provide the best dust collection, so don't skimp on the glue here.

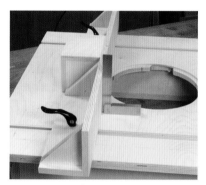

After installing the cam clamps, lock the fence in place on the top and check for square. If adjustment is necessary, you can do it by sanding the base or adding thin shims. You don't want to add shims behind the fence faces because they're moving parts. Adjust the base.

work, or worse, allowing your wood to hang up on a brad head during an operation.

Down & Dirty Fence

The fence is also absurdly simple to make. Accuracy is important to make sure it sits square to the tabletop, but other than that, it's brads and glue.

Start construction on the fence by cutting out the base, sub-face, faces and braces. All but the braces are very straightforward. The braces are actually triangles. The best method is to rip a piece of plywood to 3" wide, then head to the miter saw. First miter both ends of the strip at a 45° angle, then reset the miter saw for a 90° cut and cut the 3" triangles from the strip. Repeat this process and you've got four braces.

The sub-face and base need to have a 3"-wide half-circle cut at the center of each piece along one edge as shown above. This space will be the opening for the router bits.

The sub-face is then glued and nailed to the base. Then glue the braces into the corner formed by the sub-face and base. Make sure to locate the braces as shown to avoid interference with any of the fence handles. I again used brad nails to hold the braces in place.

For the router table to be as useful as possible it needs dust collection. This is achieved by building a simple hood to surround the bit opening in the fence. Drill a hole in the hood back piece. Adjust the hole size to fit your dust collection hose, usually 1¼" in diameter.

Then attach the hood sides to the hood back, holding the sides flush to the top edge of the back. Then add the top to the box.

The next step is to locate and drill the holes for the cam clamps that hold the fence to the table and for the knobs that hold the faces. Place the fence assembly over the table and orient the cam clamp holes so they fall in the center of the T-tracks in the top. There can be a little bit of play, but not too much.

Secure the fence to the table with the cam clamps so it seats tightly. Use an engineer's square to check the fence against the top. If it's not square you need to adjust the base slightly, either by shimming or removing material from the underside of the fence base to make it square.

Next, drill the holes for the fence knobs, again avoiding the braces so the knobs can be easily turned. The holes should be 2" up from the tabletop.

The fence faces are next. To allow the best fence clearance near the bit, I beveled the inside lip of each of the faces at 45°. Next you

Seen from the front, the fence faces have been grooved for the T-tracks, and the clearance holes to attach and adjust the faces are drilled. Note that the face slot shows the rough edges from the overlapping holes made on the drill press. A few minutes with a file and some sandpaper will clean up the slots so the bolt will move smoothly.

After drilling clearance holes, you can locate the holes in the fence faces and add the knobs.

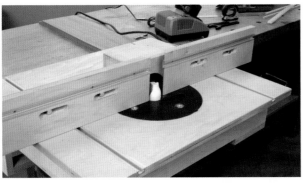

Here you can see the fences in place and the fence attached and ready to run. The T-tracks in the fence faces can be used for featherboards and you can use them to attach a simple guard to keep your hands a safe distance from the bit.

The support brace (customized for my bench vise) holds the router top firmly in place with plenty of clearance (and no wasted space).

need to rout two, 2½"-wide stepped slots in the front of each fence face. These will allow the faces to be moved left-to-right to accommodate different bit sizes.

The easiest way to do this is on a router table, but if you're building your first, you can use a drill press with two different bits. Use a ½"-diameter Forstner bit to first cut a ¼"-deep slot. Then change to a 5/16"-diameter bit to drill through to the back of the fence face. This will create a slot that will let a ½"-hex-head bolt drop into the slot, recessing the head, but capturing the sides of the bolt head to keep it from spinning.

I also added a T-slot fixture to the front of each face. This allows you to attach featherboards, a guard to protect your fingers and other guides. Again, you can use a router or your dado set in the table saw to make the slot (about 1" down from the top of the fence).

Attach the fence faces using the bolts, washers and knobs.

The Mounting Support

To make the whole thing work, you need to be able to secure the table in your bench vise, but still have access to the router motor. We used a U-shaped support screwed to the sides of the table. The actual size of the support will depend on your bench vise, but you

want the tabletop to rest on the vise as much as possible. In fact, if you can also get the top to rest on the vise at the rear of the table, that's even better support. Our larger router forced us to move the support all the way to the rear of the table. This is something else that can be individualized on your table.

You'll see in the photo that we used two support braces to catch the vise at both the top and bottom of the jaws for more support. Your vise may require a different arrangement, so give it a test run to make sure it's held tight.

Finishing Touches

With the support mounted you can put your table to work. But you may want to add a step – finishing. While a bare plywood surface will perform reasonably well, a slicker surface will make things move easier. You can add a topcoat of spray-on lacquer (as we did), or simply add a coat of oil, polyurethane or shellac.

Some other simple additions for your table can include some shop-made featherboards (that will fit nicely in the T-tracks on the fence face) and if you're really industrious, you could actually add a couple of storage drawers to either side of the opening in the top. Customize the project to meet your needs.

Ultimate Miter Saw Stand

by Jim Stuard

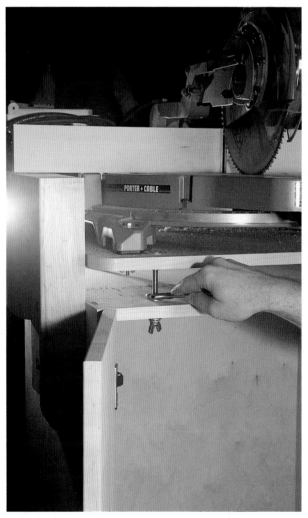

Adjusting the height of the saw is as easy as loosening the wing nuts inside the cabinet and using the jam nuts on top of the cabinet to raise or lower the saw until it's flush with the two wing assemblies.

W hen I worked in professional shops, there was always a miter saw on some kind of cart. The less-organized shops put the saw on the nearest work cart. It didn't take up much space, but it wasn't as useful as it should be. The better shops mounted the miter saw to a rolling cart and attached permanent wings to support long pieces and to hold a fence with stops for doing repetitive cuts. This setup was useful, but it took up a lot of space.

What I had in mind for Popular Woodworking's shop would have a dead-on stop system and folding wings so the stand would take up less space. The top of this stand adjusts up and down so you can line up the saw's table with the wings. (In fact, the adjustable table allows you to use a drill press or a mortiser on this stand.) It has on-board dust collection that turns itself on and off. And the kicker to the whole thing is that the cart is made from one sheet each of ¾" and ½" plywood, with some solid wood trim.

Begin construction by cutting the parts out according to the cutting list and using the optimization diagram. You'll notice that the case top is in two pieces on the optimization diagram. That's because you have to edge-glue the plywood together, then cut it to size. There isn't much scrap on this project.

One Quick Cabinet

Begin by building the cabinet. To join the sides to the top and bottom, first cut ½" x ¾" rabbets in the top and bottom edges of the sides. To hold the back, cut ½" x ½" rabbets in the back edges of the sides, top and bottom pieces. Now assemble the case. An old trade secret is to lay the case face down on your assembly bench. This way you can ensure the joint at the inside of the rabbet is flush all around. Set each joint with a couple nails, then screw the case together. Check your cabinet for squareness and make sure the back fits snugly. Attach the back with screws. Flush up the front edges of the cabinet with a plane and apply iron-on birch veneer tape. File the tape flush, sand the cabinet and mount the casters.

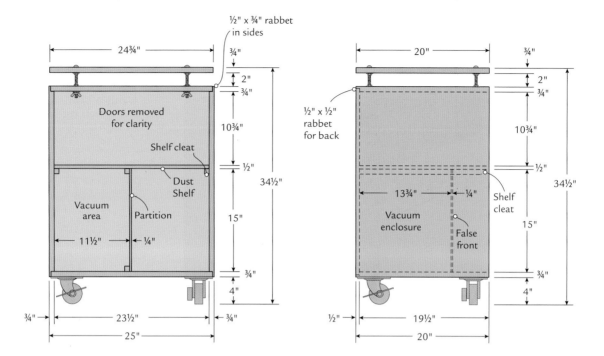

½" x ¾" rabbet in sides

24¾"

¾"
2"
¾"
10¾"
½"
15"
¾"
4"
34½"

Doors removed for clarity

Shelf cleat

Dust Shelf

Vacuum area

Partition

11½"   ¼"

¾"   23½"   ¾"
25"

ELEVATION

20"

¾"
2"
¾"
10¾"
½"
15"
¾"
4"
34½"

½" x ½" rabbet for back

Vacuum enclosure

13¾"   ¼"

Shelf cleat

False front

½"   19½"
20"

PROFILE

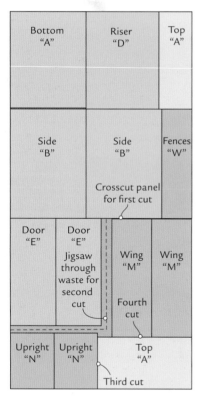

Bottom "A"	Riser "D"	Top "A"
Side "B"	Side "B"	Fences "W"
	Crosscut panel for first cut	
Door "E"	Door "E" Jigsaw through waste for second cut	Wing "M" · Wing "M"
		Fourth cut
Upright "N"	Upright "N"	Top "A"
	Third cut	

OPTIMIZATION DIAGRAM

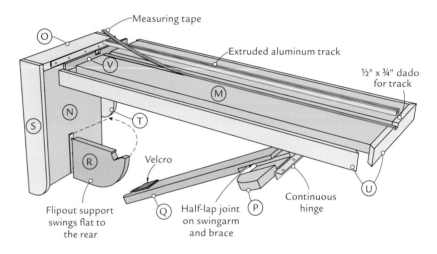

Measuring tape

Extruded aluminum track

O

V

M

S

N

T

½" x ¾" dado for track

R

Q

Velcro

Half-lap joint on swingarm and brace

P

Continuous hinge

U

Flipout support swings flat to the rear

DETAIL OF WING

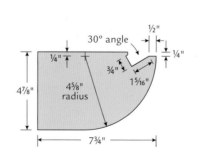

30° angle

½"

¼"

¼"

¾"   1⁵⁄₁₆"

4⅞"

4⅝" radius

7¾"

FLIP-OUT SUPPORT

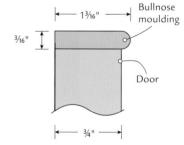

1³⁄₁₆"

Bullnose moulding

³⁄₁₆"

Door

¾"

DETAIL OF DOOR TRIM

An Adjustable Saw Platform

Now is a good time to mount the leveling riser (or platform) to your cabinet and get the miter saw set up. First cut a 1½" radius on the corners of the riser. Make sure this cut is square so that you can apply veneer tape without too much trouble. Ironing on veneer tape to the riser in one piece is a real challenge, but it looks great.

When the riser is ready, center it on top of the case and clamp it in place. Place your miter saw in the center of the riser. With a pencil, trace the locations of your saw's feet onto the riser. Also trace the holes in the machine's feet that you'll use to mount the saw to the riser. This is important because the riser floats over the case on four bolts, which allows you to adjust the saw up and down. Now mark locations for the bolts that attach the riser to the case. Be sure to keep the bolts as close as you can to the feet without them interfering with each other.

When you've marked the locations for the riser bolts, drill your holes completely through the riser and the top of the case. Hold a piece of scrap inside the case where the drill will come out to minimize tearout. Now ream out the holes a little to ease the riser adjustment.

Remove the riser from the case and drill the holes for mounting the saw. Now you can mount the riser to the case (see the list of hardware you need below). Put the bolt through the fender washer, then into the hole in the riser. Put another flat washer on the other side of the riser with a jam nut to set the bolt in place. Run a jam nut up the bolt, leaving a 2" gap between the riser and the loose jam nut. Place washers over the holes in the case and set the riser in place.

On the underside of the case, put a flat washer on the bolt, followed by a lock washer and wing nut. When you want to adjust

Hardware List

Leveling riser

4-4½" x ⅜" stove bolts (coarse thread)

4-½"x1½" fender washers

12-⅜" flat washers

4-⅜" lock washers

4-⅜" wing nuts (coarse thread)

8-⅜" jam nuts (coarse thread)

Case

4-4"casters w/locking wheels

16-½" x #10 panhead sheet-metal screws

16-¼" lock washers

1-six-outlet plug strip

Doors

4-130° European-style cup hinges

Wing supports and fence

8-2"x¼"-20 hex-head bolts

16-¼" flat washers

8-¼" lock washers

8-¼"-20 wing nuts

2-36" continuous hinge

3-36" T-track

1-L to R reading tape (72")

1-R to L reading tape (72")

2-2" square sets of Velcro (hooks and loops)

Stop

1-¼"-20 star knob

1-1½"x¼"-20 hex-head bolt

1-¼" flat washer

Saw (fastening to leveling support)

4-2½"x¼"-20 hex-head bolts

8-¼" flat washers

4-¼" lock washers

4-¼"-20 wing nuts

Ultimate Miter Saw Stand

NO.	LTR	ITEM	DIMENSIONS (INCHES)			MATERIAL
			T	W	L	
Cabinet						
2	A	Top & bottom	¾	20	24½	Plywood
2	B	Sides	¾	20	27¾	Plywood
1	C	Back	½	24½	27¼	Plywood
1	D	Leveling riser	¾	20	24¾	Plywood
2	E	Doors*	¾	12¹⁄₁₆	27⅜	Plywood
1	F	Door trim	³⁄₁₆	1³⁄₁₆	192	Solid wood
1	G	Shelf	½	19½	23½	Plywood
2	H	Shelf cleats	¾	¾	19	Solid wood
1	I	Partition	¼	15	14	Plywood
1	J	False front	¼	15	11½	Plywood
2	K	Cleats	¾	¾	13¾	Solid wood
1	L	Cleat	¾	¾	5	Solid wood
Wings						
2	M	Wings	¾	10⅜	30	Plywood
2	N	Uprights	¾	11½	14¼	Plywood
2	O	Upright ledges	¾	2¾	11½	Solid wood
2	P	Swingarm braces	¾	4	10⅜	Solid wood
2	Q	Swingarms	¾	3	20	Solid wood
2	R	Flip-out supports	¾	4⅞	7¾	Solid wood
2	S	Front brackets	½	2¾	15	Solid wood
2	T	Rear brackets	½	2¾	10	Solid wood
1	U	Wing trim	½	1½	15'	Solid wood
1	V	Edge trim	¼	1³⁄₁₆	24	Solid wood
2	W	Fences	¾	3	16¼	Plywood
1	X	Stop block	¾	2	3	Solid wood

* Size before applying door trim.

The easiest way to assemble the wing is to attach the hinge to the upright assembly. Then remove it and attach it to the wing. Clamp the upright in a vise and reattach everything. Make sure to mark each hinge's location or you'll mess up how some parts go together.

the riser height, simply loosen the wing nuts and adjust the jam nut against the case top to raise or lower the riser.

To complete the case, build and hang the plywood doors. Nail a 1³⁄₁₆" solid maple edge with a bullnose profile to the edges.

Use European hinges (sometimes called concealed hinges) on your doors. I'm fond of a $30 jig that easily locates the holes for the hinges and the mounting plates (Euro-Eze, item #905-599, $41.99 from Woodworker's Supply, 800-645-9292 or www.woodworker. com). Drill the hinges' cup holes about 4" in from the top and bottom of the case.

Automatic Vacuum

Now mount the saw and outfit the cabinet with the vacuum and electrical parts. When the saw and vacuum are hooked up properly, the vacuum will come on automatically when you turn the saw on (thanks to the "i-socket 110m Tool and Vacuum Switch," #20890, $39.99 from Rockler, 800-279-4441 or www.rockler.com), and it will turn off a few seconds after you finish your cut.

Start by drilling two 2" holes in the back near the bottom of the case. One hole is for the vacuum hose (locate it according to your vacuum). The other is for the wiring. I enclosed the vacuum in a partition made from two pieces of plywood and the shelf. The shelf height in the drawing works for most small two-gallon vacuums. Lay out the height of the bottom edge of the shelf. Mount a pair of cleats to these lines. Screw the shelf in from the top.

Now screw cleats to the inside of the case to make the partition and false front that conceals the vacuum. Notch your plywood pieces to wrap around the shelf cleat and the power cord for the

vacuum. Turn the vacuum's switch to "on," place it in the new cubby and hook up the vacuum's hose to the saw through a hole in the back.

Screw an outlet strip to the bottom of the case and run the strip's cord through a hole in the back. Plug the Rockler Vacuum Switch into the outlet strip and plug in the saw. Now screw the partition and false front in place to conceal the vacuum.

Huge Wings

The wings are the last thing to do. Begin by gluing and nailing ¼"-thick solid wood edge trim to one end of the wings. This edging gives the piano hinge some meat to bite into. Finish the wings by applying the ½" x 1½" trim to the other three edges.

Study the diagram on page 88 to see how the wings are supported. First apply the upright ledges to the uprights. Cut the 2" radii on the brackets and then attach them in place.

Cut the swing arms, braces and flip-out supports. The swing arm and brace need a half-lap joint that makes a "T" shape. Attach the continuous hinge to the top of the "T." The best way to cut this joint is with a dado head in a table saw. Cut a ¾" x ¾" notch on the end of the swing arms to mate with the flip-out support.

The last thing to do to the arms is to round off the corners: 1" on the ends and 3½" on the brackets. Now mount the swing-arm assemblies to the underside of the wings using a 10" piece of continuous hinge, with the notched end of the swing arm ¼" in from the point where the wing meets the case. To keep everything from flopping around when the arms are down, use adhesive-backed Velcro between the swing arms and wings. Reinforce the Velcro's adhesive with staples.

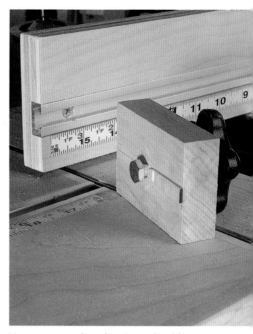

There is a lot of aluminum channel out there these days, but I chose this T-track because a ¼"-20 bolt head will fit in the channel. It comes predrilled and countersunk from Woodcraft (item #TTK6, $13.99, 800-535-4482 or www.woodcraft.com) and machines nicely. You'll probably have to file down some screws that pop out from the other side.

Here you can see how the stop works with the fence system. Note the thin guide strip that prevents your stop from wobbling as you set it.

Finish the wings by cutting a ½" x ¾" dado down the middle of the wing for the extruded aluminum channel for the stop. Next to that dado, cut a second shallow dado that's ½" wide and as deep as your stick-on measuring tape is thick. Cut the aluminum channel to length and screw it in place.

Now concentrate on the flip-out supports. After cutting out the mating notches for the swing arms, cut a ³⁄₁₆" x ⅝" rabbet into the end of the support to accept a 4¾"-long piece of continuous hinge. Lay out and mount the support to the upright, centered and flush to the bottom edge.

The last step on the wings is to attach the wing assembly to the upright. Do this carefully so that the surface of the wing is flush with the upright ledge. Now, if everything's OK, your wings should lock flush and square to the upright. If you didn't get it right the first time, add a flat-head screw to the inside of each notch and you will be able to adjust the height of the wing.

To attach the wing assemblies, temporarily remove the saw/riser assembly and remove the wing from the upright assembly. Cut a spacer that's 2¾" plus the height of the saw's table. Clamp the spacer flush to the upright ledge. Lay the wing assembly on the edge of the case. On the saw/riser assembly, measure from the front edge of the riser to the saw fence. Subtract 1¾" from that number and mark it on the case, measuring from the front. This is where the upright should be mounted. It accounts for the thickness of the ¾" saw fence and the distance from the center of the stop to the fence. Mount the upright with the hardware listed. Make sure to counterbore the bolt heads and washers. This allows the flip-out support to fold flat against the upright. Re-attach the wings and flush the saw table up to the wings by resting a straight piece of lumber across the wings. Adjust the saw's height and lock it down.

The last step is to make the fences and the stop, and to attach the tapes. First rip a couple of 3½"-wide sections of plywood from your scrap. Then cut them to 1" longer than the distance from the blade to the outside edge of the upright. That should be about 16¼", as long as your saw is centered correctly on the base.

Cut ½" x ¾" dados 1" to the center from one edge. The edge that the dado is closest to is the bottom edge. Repeat the ½" dado for the tape so it's above the dado. Glue in a 4"-long filler into the groove at the end next to the blade and attach a length of aluminum channel to fill the remaining length. Make a mirror part for the other side. This keeps your hands at least 4" away from the blade – a safe distance. Attach the fences by lowering the saw (as if you were making a cut) and butting each fence against the blade. Clamp the fence pieces there and screw them in place.

Cut the measuring tape to 16" and stick it in place. Use a square block to index off the 16" marks and, after cutting the tapes to length (around 46"), stick them in place, butting the end up against the block on each side of the saw blade.

Finally, make the stop that runs in the channel. The stop is a simple 2" x 3" block with a ¼" hole in it. Make a guide strip that's about ⁵⁄₁₆" x ¹⁄₁₆". It's easier if you make the strip a little thick and plane it down to the ¹⁄₁₆" thickness. Drill the ¼" hole through and test it with a bolt and star knob.

Chapter Fourteen

Drill Press Table

by Steve Shanesy

There are all manner of drill press tables and fences, from a simple 2x4 clamped to the machine's cast iron table to ones with gadgets and gizmos galore. The latter is not my style, so when the time came to replace my drill press table the list of requirements was short:

• *Accuracy.* The table must be flat and stay flat, and the fence must be square to the table.

• *Ease of use.* My prior table had a fence fixed to the table itself, so every fence adjustment required loosening and tightening F-style clamps to the irregular bottom of the cast iron table.

• *Longevity.* Though I tried not to, I eventually fouled my old table by drilling into it too many times.

• *Workholding.* There are times when I need to clamp down my work but normal clamps won't reach.

With these issues in mind, I developed this drill press table.

Choose Your Materials

I decided to use MDF for the table because it is flat and stable. Plywood is another option so long as it's flat (which is typically the case only in the highest grades). I dismissed a melamine-clad particleboard because the surface is too slippery. The fence is cut from a clear section of a 2x4 that I jointed straight and square. A piece of plywood is screwed to the bottom of the fence. The plywood itself is clamped to the MDF table. T-track and T-bolts are used for fence adjustment and securing it to the table. An additional piece of T-track is set closer to the front of the table for workholding when the need arises. Just about any commercially available T-track based hold-down can be used.

Make the Table

My table is 18" x 28" – a generous size for most work. If you are challenged for space in your shop you may want to scale it down. I should also note that my drill press has an 18" swing. If your drill press is smaller, you'll need to shorten the amount of travel for the fence.

TAKE THE PLUNGE. I used a plunge router with a fence to cut the ¾"-wide by ½"-deep grooves for the T-track. I also clamped a piece of stock to the table to act as a stop for the router cut.

Below the table surface is a second piece of MDF that is 16" x 23", which I'll call a sub-table. The sub-table gets screwed on later but its main purpose is to provide more thickness to the table in order to securely screw down the T-track. Set the sub-table aside for now.

First up on the table was routing the grooves for the T-track. My T-track is ¾" wide x ½" thick. When routing these grooves, make them a hair deeper than the T-track's thickness. I routed the two grooves for the fence about 4¼" in from each side and made them 5¾" long, as measured from the back edge. To cut the grooves I used a plunge router with a fence attached.

The groove for the workholding piece of T-track is routed at about a 45° angle. Its placement is somewhat arbitrary, but you can use the drawing to see where I positioned mine. Again, this piece

Supplies

Rockler Woodworking and Hardware

- Rockler.com or 800-279-4441

1 Universal T-track, 2' length
#22104, $14.99

2 T-bolts, 1½", #38002, $3.99 (pkg of 5)

2 T-bolt knobs, #23838, $.79

Prices correct at time of publication.

Drill Press Table

NO.	ITEM	DIMENSIONS (INCHES)			MATERIAL
		T	W	L	
1	Table	¾	18	28	MDF
1	Sub-table	¾	16	23	MDF
1	Table insert	¾	4¾ dia.		MDF
1	Fence	1⅜	2¾	27½	Pine
1	Fence base	¾	3½	24½	Plywood

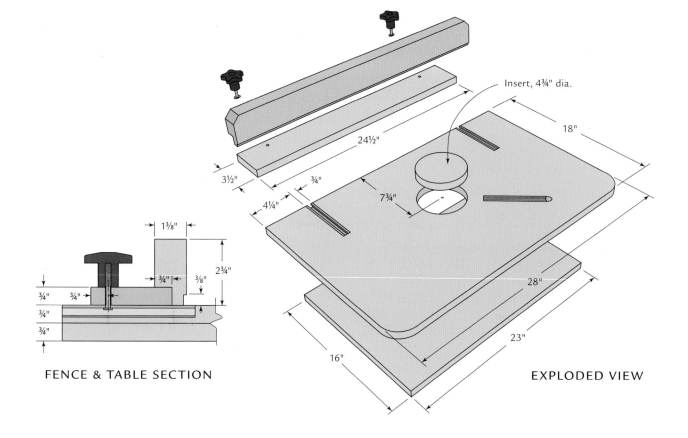

FENCE & TABLE SECTION

EXPLODED VIEW

LET 'ER FLY. The large hole in the table is made using a fly cutter. Keep your hands well away from the spinning cutter and be careful using this tool.

is about 5¾" long, but make your groove slightly longer so you can insert a T-bolt in the track.

Next, I made a 4¾"-diameter hole using a fly cutter. It is centered side to side on the table, and 7¾" from the back edge. In this hole I drop in a like-sized insert that can easily be replaced as needed – that remedies the problem of ruining the table from repeatedly drilling into it. To make the insert I simply drew the circle using a compass and carefully cut out the circle on the band saw. A few minutes of sanding the outside edge and the fit was good.

Before assembling all the table parts I rounded the front corners, cutting a 2" radius using the band saw.

To complete the table, screw the sub-table to the table from below. Keep the screw locations away from the center area and the T-track grooves. Then screw the T-track in place and pop the round insert into the table. At this stage, you can go ahead and bolt the table assembly to the cast iron table of the drill press.

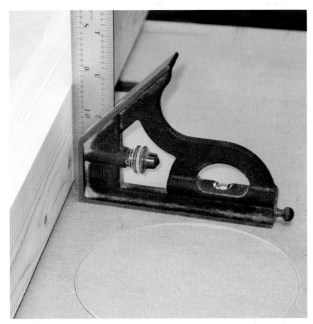

SQUARE IS A MUST. Your fence and table must be square so check it carefully.

Make the Fence

Before you start, make sure the fence material is dead flat and square all around. As mentioned earlier, I used a clear piece of 2x4 that I milled flat and square using a jointer and planer . Next, cut a piece of plywood 3½" wide and about as long as the fence. Designate what will be the face of the fence and the back. On the bottom back edge, cut a rabbet about ¾" wide and as deep as the plywood is thick. Try to get everything nice and square – both the plywood edge and the rabbet. Now, on the bottom front face, cut a small rabbet about ⅛" deep and ⅜" wide. Before you screw the plywood into the rabbet on the fence, clip the upper corners of the ends of the fence. It's more user-friendly and looks nice.

Once the fence is screwed together, set it on the drill press table and carefully compare the fence face to the table to determine if it is indeed square. If it's out even slightly, here's the fix: Go to your jointer (make sure the jointer fence is dead square to the table) and, with the plywood base of the fence against the jointer fence, take a light jointer pass over the face of the drill press's fence face. This should correct any irregularity and true it up. Go back to the drill press table and check it again. If square, it's done.

Then, set the fence above the T-track so it's centered side to side. Mark the centers of the track slots on the plywood base of the fence. Then drill clearance holes for the T-bolts through the plywood in locations away from the fence that will allow the knobs to turn freely.

There are a few additional features on this fence. That shallow rabbet you made on the lower front will allow a ¼"-thick sacrificial board to slide in and still allow space for wood chips so the stock stays tight against the fence. Also, you can turn the fence around so that the plywood edge faces the front. This low fence is perfect for drilling small holes close to the edge of a board. This low fence also prevents the drill press chuck from hitting the fence before the bit can be sufficiently lowered into the work.

ROUND UP YOUR INSERT. To make the round insert for the table, simply draw the circle with a compass, then carefully cut it out at the band saw.

THE FIX IS IN. You can always square up the drill press fence by taking a pass over your jointer after making sure the jointer fence is square.

Chapter Fifteen

Swinging Outfeed Table

by Eric Hedberg

W ho says that table saws aren't "hip?" This version of an outfeed table puts a little swing in one of the most useful but problematic tools in my shop, and like Duke Ellington says: "It don't mean a thing if it ain't got that swing." In my cramped shop, this is especially true. Wall space has premium value, and precious little is available to hang accessories and supplies on. The only thing more precious is my floor space.

My table saw at home is a classic contractor saw. During any rip, the pieces run off the end of the table and drop on the motor. This is not exactly safe, nor good for the components for my projects. I needed a short outfeed table for most of my work, but on the long rips or bigger panels, I needed a table with more space. You can attach an outfeed table to most table saws, whether it's a contractor saw like mine or a cabinet saw like the one in the Popular Woodworking shop shown here. By combining a few metal brackets, a piano hinge and a handful of nuts and bolts with my own version of a drop leaf table, I came up with my swingin' new outfeed table that will work on almost any table saw to provide more workspace.

Getting in the Swing of Things

The outfeed table is made up of two pieces. The short table is 12" x 40". The swing table is 24" x 40". They can be made of any suitable panel material such as Baltic birch plywood or melamine. Cut the tops to size (don't you wish you had an outfeed table?). A circular saw is fine, as absolute squareness is not necessary for them to function properly.

There are some minor steps to fit the short table to your saw. Part of that will be determined when you attach the mounting hardware to your saw. Each saw will require slightly different adjustments to mount the short table. You may need to leave more or less room between the saw and the short table's aprons, depending on the mounting procedure. A ¾" x ⅛" rabbet was necessary to fit the table snug against the saw top on the Powermatic saw shown

on page 97. Also, you'll want to rout a couple of grooves to extend the miter gauge slots into the short table. Otherwise your miter gauge bar will be blocked by the short table.

When you've finished the tabletops, it's time to cut the parts for the apron pieces. The apron can be made from any suitable soft/hardwood or even plywood stock you have available.

The legs are 1½" x 1½" and cut to a length appropriate for your table saw. Leg levelers, available from any hardware store or home center, added to the tips of all four legs allow you to easily make fine adjustments to the table height for a perfect match for your saw's table.

Putting It All Together

Before assembling the aprons, mount the table saw hardware on the saw according to the directions included with the hardware. Center the front apron piece and mark locations for the brackets and screws. Remember to allow for the ¾" top when aligning the apron piece to the saw's tabletop. Screw the brackets to the apron and tighten the bolts on the table saw. You can make adjustments at this stage to get the height just right without dealing with the completed table.

Now the fun starts. I used my pocket-hole jig and used pocket screws to assemble the small table and apron. Pocket screws are quick and easy to use and sufficiently strong to hold things together. If you like your biscuits, go for it. Just about any table-assembly method will work fine.

The back edge of the large tabletop will overhang the apron by 6". This gives clearance for the legs of the drop leaf. I screwed the permanent legs to the inside of the apron and attached the folding legs using the folding table leg brackets (Rockler, item #39505, $15.99 per pair, 800-279-4441 or www.rockler.com). The folding legs are staggered to allow them to fold up. You can space them as you choose, but about ½" between them is just fine. Install the locking hinges first and then the legs. Make sure they swing in the correct direction.

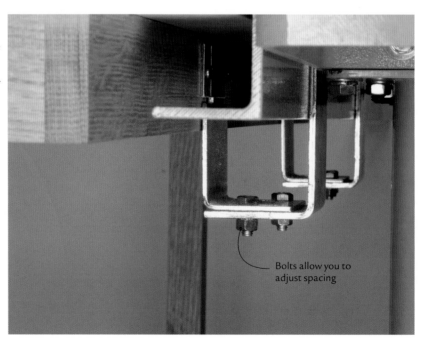

By installing separate brackets on the outfeed apron and the table saw's rear rail, the outfeed can be adjusted for both height and distance in relation to the rear edge of the saw's table.

Bolts allow you to adjust spacing

With everything upside down on your bench, slide the swing part of the outfeed table up to the mating edge on the assembled short table. Install a piano hinge to the underside of the two tables, bridging the gap. Be careful to center the barrel of the hinge on the gap. When the swing table is opened, the hinge will be at a 90° angle.

Now hang the assembly on the saw. This is a good time to tune up the leg lengths and bracket adjustments. Lift the assembly off the saw to make these adjustments.

Hitting the Floor

When everything looks satisfactory, reinstall the assembly on the back of your table saw. Check the assembled outfeed table for operation and seal and finish the table as you choose. Most of the time you will probably, like me, find the short outfeed table sufficient, but when those panels and long pieces show up, your outfeed table will be ready to swing into action at a moment's notice.

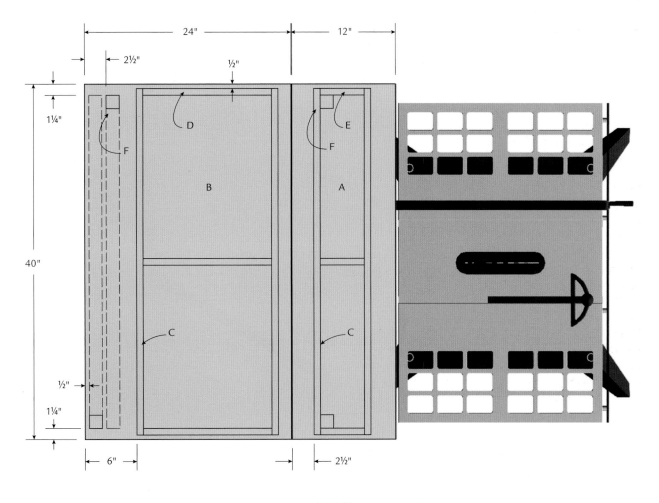

PLAN

Swinging Outfeed Table

NO.	LET.	ITEM	DIMENSIONS (INCHES)			MATERIAL
			T	W	L	
1	A	Short table	¾	12	40	Plywood
1	B	Swing table	¾	24	40	Plywood
4	C	Aprons	¾	2¼	39	Oak
3	D	Aprons	¾	21¼	15	Oak
3	E	Aprons	¾	2¼	5⅛	Oak
4	F	Legs	1½	1½	32-36	Oak

Chapter Sixteen

Shooting Boards

by Graham Blackburn

There was a time, before the introduction of power tools, when the handplane was the very icon of woodworking. Nowadays of course, woodworking is often represented by the table saw and the electric router (among many other power tools). But as more and more woodworkers rediscover the pleasure — not to mention the economies, increased possibilities and safety — of incorporating various hand tools and techniques into their woodworking practices, there is a renewed interest in traditional woodworking.

Today's amateur woodworker is presented with a growing array of ever-better designed hand tools that often rival the products of such legendary firms as Norris, Preston and even early Stanley products. There is also an increasing amount of information about how to restore, fettle and sharpen these tools.

But whether you buy a brand-new handplane, an expensive model from the beginning of the 20th century, an antique wooden tool or even a lesser-quality modern item, learning how to condition and prepare the tool itself is only half the equation. The other half is the technique of using the tool. The best-conditioned and most expensive plane in the world may well produce nothing but frustration if you remain ignorant of how best to use it.

The Missing Half

It used to be commonly understood that the term "hand-tool use" is rarely synonymous with the term "freehand use." Except perhaps for carvers, most traditional woodworkers would no more consider using a handplane freehand than would today's woodworkers consider using a table saw or other power tool without some form of fence or guide. Indeed, these things are invariably built into the power tool itself.

But the vast majority of handplanes — and there is an enormous range of handplanes — need some external form of guidance if consistency and accuracy are to be achieved.

While some planes, including fillisters and moulding planes, are equipped with a fence and even a depth stop, there is seldom little else that is built in to guarantee accuracy.

This is especially the case with the most common tools: the so-called bench planes. These are the planes used for dimension-

Track for "chute" plane

Metal base

Adjustable stop (fence) for clamping workpiece at desired angle to plane.

STANLEY SHOOTING BOARD.
The No. 52 (which included the plane and cast iron shooting board) was offered from 1909-1943. If you can find a set today in good shape, it is likely to cost upward of $1,000. However, the setup does an excellent job of squaring edges.

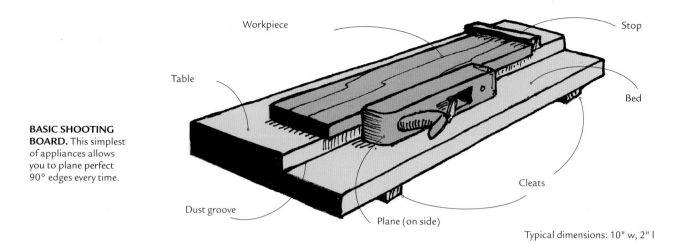

BASIC SHOOTING BOARD. This simplest of appliances allows you to plane perfect 90° edges every time.

Workpiece

Table

Stop

Bed

Cleats

Dust groove

Plane (on side)

Typical dimensions: 10" w, 2" l

ing, flattening, squaring and even final finishing of the workpiece. They include jack planes, fore planes and jointer planes, in all their varieties.

Accurate Edges

When it comes to preparing edges, the essential adjunct to all these planes is some form of shooting board. That this device is often unfamiliar to many woodworkers is because, apart from a few relatively rare (and now very expensive collector's items such as the Stanley Chute Board), these items were invariably user-made rather than manufactured and store-bought.

The good news is that making your own shooting board and learning how to use it is far from difficult.

If you secure a workpiece in the vise with the edge to be planed uppermost, you can easily run a plane along this edge. But, depending on the thickness of the edge, you may find it difficult to maintain the plane at a perfect 90° angle to the face of the board. On the other hand, if you place the board flat on its face and use the plane on its side — assuming the side of the plane is perfectly square to its sole and the surface of the bench is perfectly flat — the edge can theoretically be planed perfectly square to the face of the board.

There are, however, two problems with the latter method. First, the board needs to be secured by stops or clamps; and second, most bench planes have irons that do not extend to the outside corners

of the sole. Using the plane on its side directly against the edge to be planed means that it is impossible to plane the entire width of the edge.

The shooting board solves both these problems, for it is really nothing more than a jig for holding any given workpiece both securely enough and high enough so that the tool can be used on its side to plane the edge at a consistently accurate angle.

Basic Shooting Board

The simplest form of shooting board consists of three pieces: a base on which the plane runs on its side; a table where the workpiece rests to raise it so the plane's iron engages the workpiece's entire edge; and a stop fixed to the table against which the workpiece is held.

Unless the shooting board is made from some form of stable plywood or particleboard, it is usual to fix transverse cleats to the bottom of the base to keep it perfectly flat.

These cleats, if carefully positioned, can also be used to secure the board on the bench, either by being hooked over the front of the bench (and possibly also over the edge of a tool well), or by being held between bench dogs.

An alternative method is to add to the underside of the base a longitudinal keel that can be held in the vise (although cleats may still be advisable to keep the board from warping).

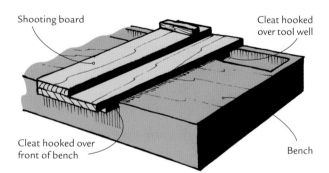

Shooting board

Cleat hooked over tool well

Cleat hooked over front of bench

Bench

CLEATS. A cleat at the near end acts as a bench hook; a second cleat, at the far end, drops into the tool well. (You could skip the far cleat if you build the shooting board from a stable materials, such as plywood.)

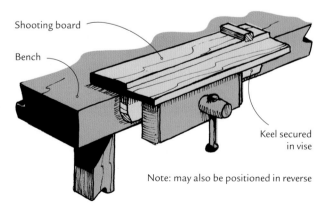

Shooting board

Bench

Keel secured in vise

Note: may also be positioned in reverse

KEEL. A keel attached on the underside of the shooting board can be secured in a vise.

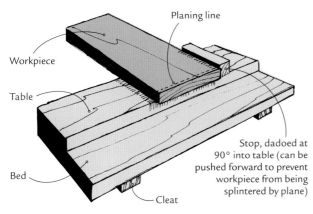

Planing line

Workpiece

Table

Bed

Cleat

Stop, dadoed at 90° into table (can be pushed forward to prevent workpiece from being splintered by plane)

STOP. To trim ends dead square, the stop must be affixed at 90° to the straight edge of the table.

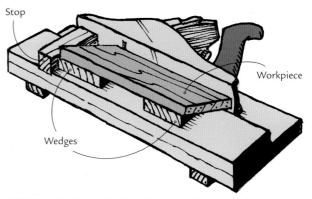

Stop

Workpiece

Wedges

OFF 90°. A basic shooting board can be used to plane edges at angles other than 90°; simply insert wedges of the needed angle under your workpiece.

The stop (the piece against which you hold the workpiece) can simply be nailed in place or wedged into a deep dado cut in the top of the shooting board base. (The latter method is, in my opinion, better because it allows you to move the stop over as its end becomes worn or damaged.)

Either way, make sure the stop is fixed at 90° to the table so the workpiece registers against it accurately for trimming ends square.

It is important that when planing you hold the workpiece so its edge overhangs the table a little; the plane is never used so that it bears against the edge of the table. Rather, it is worked to a line marked on the workpiece. Nevertheless, it is good practice to plane a small dust groove on the bottom edge of the table where it contacts the bed to prevent any build-up from forcing the plane away from the work.

No matter how carefully you make the shooting board, it cannot do its job if your plane's sole is not perfectly perpendicular to the side on which it is run.

Most right-handed woodworkers prefer to use a plane on its right side, so the stop and table are fixed to the left side of the shooting board's bed. If you are left-handed, reverse the positions and run the plane on its left side.

In the days when plane bodies were all wood, care had to be taken when periodically shooting the sole of the plane so it remained perfectly square to the sides. (You cannot plane anything flatter than the flatness of a plane's sole.)

This is not hard to do with a wooden plane, but metal-bodied planes present a different problem. Better-made planes may well have square soles, but if it is necessary to flatten the sole, be sure to maintain perpendicularity with the sides – particularly for the side that will run on the board.

Once you understand the principles behind a simple shooting board used to achieve a perfectly square edge, consider the following varieties.

Angled Edges

You may need to plane edges at angles other than 90°. You can do this easily with a basic shooting board simply by altering the angle of the table on which the workpiece rests. The simplest way to do this is to place appropriately angled wedges under the workpiece. Alternatively, temporarily tack a narrow strip to the back of the table.

A slightly more involved method, but one that will give you more choice and security in the long run, is to hinge the front edge of the table to its bed. Include some form of thumbscrew-fixed height-adjustment to the back edge to keep the angle from changing in use.

Angled Ends

While a perfectly square stop is useful for shooting the end of a workpiece at 90° to its length, other angles may sometimes be

To trim ends of mouldings, place your work on proper side of stop. Always plane into the profile.

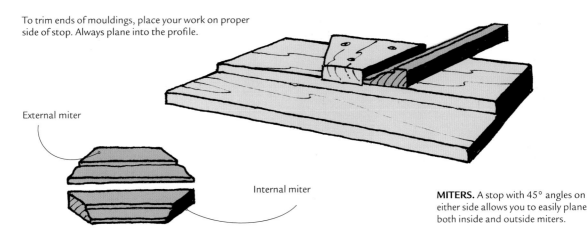

External miter

Internal miter

MITERS. A stop with 45° angles on either side allows you to easily plane both inside and outside miters.

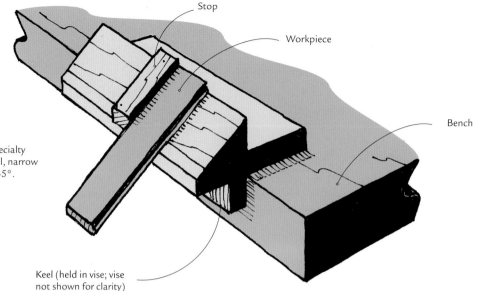

DONKEY'S EAR. This specialty appliance for shooting tall, narrow miters has a bed fixed at 45°.

Stop

Workpiece

Bench

Keel (held in vise; vise not shown for clarity)

required. These can be easily achieved with the use of an auxiliary wedge-shaped piece inserted between the stop and the workpiece. Furthermore, if used in combination with any of the previous methods for shooting angled edges, the shooting board can be turned into a device for accurately planing the ends of mitered and splayed work.

Miters

Trimming miters freehand is risky. If you have to trim relatively narrow mitered pieces such as moulding, make a shooting board that consists of a bed and a table as before, but fix a stop, cut at 45° on both sides, in the center of the table's length. That way, you will be able to plane into internal and external miters without risk of splintering the ends.

When you need to trim tall narrow miters, such as those at the ends of skirting, moulded baseboards, cornices or plinths, you need the quaintly named donkey's ear shooting board. It is essentially the same as a regular shooting board except that the table is at a fixed 45° angle and the stop is placed in the center of its length.

Because such pieces to be trimmed are frequently quite long, the shooting board must be used close to the front edge of the bench. This typically means that it will be held by a longitudinal keel in the face vise.

Miter Shooting Block

Although by definition not strictly a shooting board, any discussion of the topic would be incomplete without mention of the miter shooting block.

This device is used for miters that are both long and wide. Its utility is derived from the broad area of support for the plane that is used to trim the workpiece (and those surfaces are commonly protected by a thin card glued to their surfaces in case the plane's

MITER BLOCK. A miter block (shown here in the left-handed orientation) was once a common commercially available appliance.

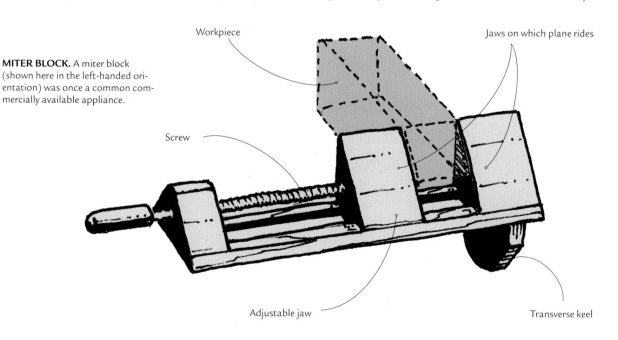

Workpiece

Jaws on which plane rides

Screw

Adjustable jaw

Transverse keel

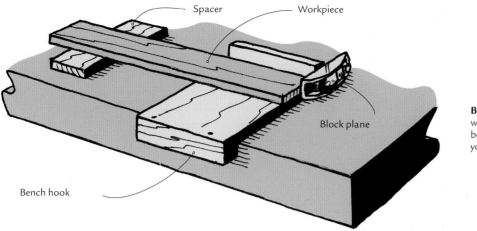

Spacer Workpiece

Block plane

Bench hook

BENCH HOOK. As long as your workbench is flat, you can use a bench hook to hold a workpiece as you shoot the end square.

iron should inadvertently travel over these parts). Once commonly manufactured in both left-and right-handed varieties, a simpler version can easily be made.

Last Thoughts

Lacking any form of shooting board, you can use a simple bench hook for trimming end grain. It will provide the two essentials: a stop for the work and an elevated edge for a plane used on its side directly on the bench.

Most bench hooks are relatively small, typically no more than 12" x 12", so the length of the workpiece that can be shot is short indeed. But using a pair of bench hooks, or even one bench hook and a spacer, is an easy way to trim the end of any board square and true.

And finally, what can you do when the workpiece is too long to be used with a shooting board? (There is, after all, a practical limit to the length you can make a shooting board.)

To paraphrase an old proverb, "if you can't take the work to a shooting board, take the shooting board to the work." Clamp a thick and rabbeted fence to the side of your plane and hold this

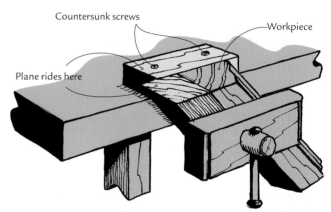

Countersunk screws Workpiece

Plane rides here

SHOP-MADE. With little ingenuity (and less fuss), you can easily make a simple miter block in your shop.

fence tightly against the workpiece (secured in a vise). This produces the same effect of keeping the sole of the plane at a consistent angle to the edge being shot. And of course, this fence can also be angled to work on edges other than those at 90°.

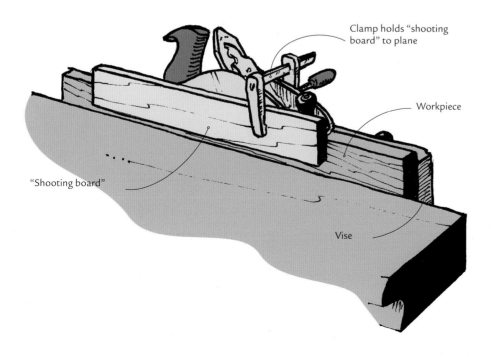

Clamp holds "shooting board" to plane

Workpiece

"Shooting board"

Vise

FENCE. If you don't have a shooting board of sufficient size to hold the work, attach a fence to the plane to hold it at the desired angle.

Wall-hung Tool Racks

by Robert W. Lang

I used to keep my hand tools in drawers in machinists' and mechanics' tool chests. My tools were organized and protected, but it wasn't very convenient. Edge tools rattled against one another as drawers opened and closed, and my layout tools were never at hand. During projects, tools stayed on the bench where they could be found, but soon were buried as my work, shavings, scraps and more tools piled up.

When I opened my first shop, I decided to make a wall-hung tool chest. Two wide doors opened off a cabinet. I designed the

doors around the tools I used regularly, and in between the doors were shelves and a bank of dovetailed drawers. It changed the way I worked. The tools had a place to live and were right at hand. If I started to see too much empty space in the inside of the doors, I knew it was time to take a break and clean up.

While the wall-hung chest functioned well, I never quite completed it. I intended to put in a latch and lock mechanism to keep the doors closed, but after a few months, I realized that I rarely closed the doors. It was like a television cabinet in most homes –

The simple start is two pieces of wood, ¾" thick x 3½" wide, of a convenient length. The back piece is longer than the front by a few inches to allow fastening to the wall. The rack is wide enough to hold tools securely, and provides a place for Shaker pegs for hanging tools.

The two pieces are separated by ½"-thick spacers, and tools drop into the space. This was a "sweet spot" for our tools and can be varied to accommodate your tools.

the doors are functional but if the TV is always on (or the tools always being used), the doors really aren't needed.

When I came to work at Woodworking Magazine, I planned to bring in my tool chest and hang it on the wall. My plan had to be aborted when I recognized that our shop's biggest blessing, an abundance of windows, didn't allow the 6' of wall space I needed. I was back to tools in drawers and odd boxes, and I pondered how to add a wall without losing any windows. I wanted the accessibility, safety and organization of the chest, but I was developing an impractical plan.

One day as I walked into the shop, I glanced to the left as I almost always do. Most of the time there will be some interesting project or part of a project or esoteric tool on Christopher Schwarz's bench. What caught my eye that morning was his simple and elegant solution to the same problem I faced. He had installed a simple rack across the window directly above his bench and it held more tools than I would have thought possible.

Recognizable as leftover baseboard, two ¾"-thick boards, about 3½" wide, were held ½" apart by wood spacers in between.

The back board was a few inches longer than the one in front, allowing it to be easily mounted to the wall, or in this case the wood casing on our window. By that afternoon, I was loading a similar rack across the window above the bench in my corner of the shop.

I was delighted at how well this simple solution solved a problem. My only reservation about hanging my tools was securing them so they wouldn't fall. When I made my tool chest, I made French-fit holders for individual tools. With the new rack, most would fit neatly within the slot between the two boards. They were handy, in sight and out of danger. A few didn't fit between the slots, so I drove a few screws and nails to hang them on the outer part of the rack.

Organization came in time. Instead of planning where each tool should go ahead of time, I started using the slotted rack as I worked, putting tools in a slot as I completed typical tasks. Before long, an organizational scheme emerged that works better than I would have planned. I also found that the slots were good for many tools, but not everything fit quite the way I wanted.

Screws and nails aren't as attractive as Shaker pegs, but function well –
especially in tight spaces and for tool-specific hanging.

The flexibility of using
the slots gives you
freedom to change the
overall arrangement as
your tools, needs, hab-
its or projects change
over time.

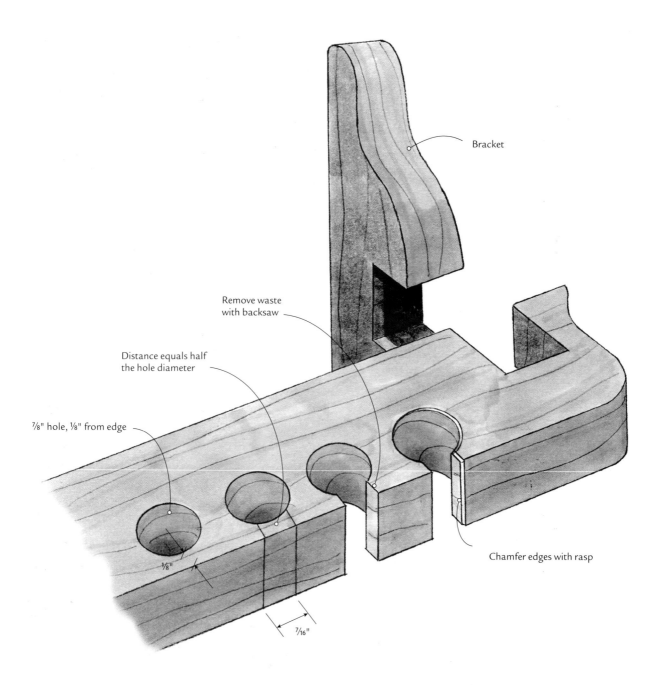

Bracket

Remove waste
with backsaw

Distance equals half
the hole diameter

7/8" hole, 1/8" from edge

1/8"

7/16"

Chamfer edges with rasp

WALL-HUNG TOOL RACK DETAIL

Above the bench at the other end of the shop, Shaker pegs began to appear on the outside of my shop mate's rack. First, a few near one end, then an entire row with hammers hanging from them. A day or two later, another row of pegs appeared above the first rack, holding more than a dozen saws. Not being a collector, I didn't need that much space – I only have four saws and five hammers, but my tool rack did need some improvements and additions.

My first addition was a simple shelf, about 4" wide that rests on band-sawn brackets. This provided a place for planes and a few other tools that I didn't want to hang, but needed at hand. The remaining problem to solve was the chisel chaos. They fit between the boards of the rack, but because they're top heavy with wide handles, they wouldn't hang straight. It bothered me to see them leaning against each other like a gang of out-of-work loafers. I wanted them standing straight – at attention and ready for action.

My solution was another shelf, held in notched brackets with a series of holes that fit the chisel handles. I experimented with some different-sized holes and various chisels and found that a 7/8" diameter worked for almost all of them. I also wanted a slot at the front of the hole so I wouldn't need to lift a chisel its entire length to get it in or out of the rack. A little more experimentation and a couple test-fittings later, and I had my final dimensions; the holes were drilled with the edge of the hole ⅛" back from the front edge of the 2"-wide board. A center-to-center distance of 1⅛" provided room to reach each handle individually.

After marking off the series of equally spaced centerlines, I stepped off one-fourth the diameter from each side of the center-lines and sawed slots from the front edge of the shelf to each hole, leaving a ⁷⁄₁₆"-wide slot connecting each hole to the edge. I used a rasp to chamfer the edges of the holes and slots, connected the shelf to the brackets, and mounted them in place. Wider chisels need a bit of a turn as they go in and out of the rack. Narrow ones slide right in. They all are held securely.

More concerned about function than decoration, I made my racks out of scrap hardwoods and didn't use a finish. A light sanding and a coat of shellac, lacquer, oil or wax would make them look nicer, but I rarely bother with doing that on something for the shop.

I considered doing some decorative carving on the brackets, but that reminded me that my carving chisels still live in canvas rolls in drawers in a nearby cabinet. I'm not a collector, but I will need a rack for 40 or 50 of them, and while I'm at it, I may as well start gathering the 30 or 40 more carving chisels that I really need. Maybe I can clear some space on the building column to the left of my bench for a row of them.

The great thing about these racks is that they are adaptable and made easily and quickly. As happened to me, once you start, you'll need another two or three as the list of necessary tools grows, and the way you work and the things you work on change. If you cross the line to "collector," you might need many more than that.

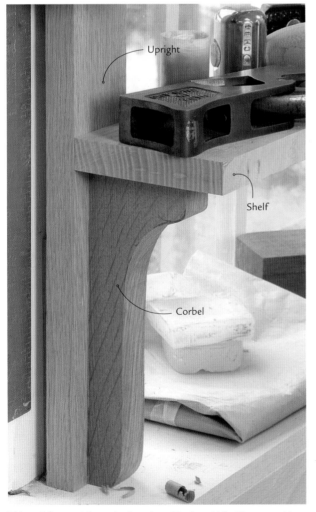

This rack has uprights at both ends and in the middle. These provide a place for brackets and corbels that can support shelves.

A ⅞"-diameter hole, ⅛" in from the edge of a 2"-wide shelf holds a variety of handle sizes. The sawn slot connecting the hole and edge allows you to hold a chisel with a blade that is wider than the handle diameter.

Practical Shop Cabinet

by Troy Sexton

One of my favorite things to do when I have free time is to tinker around my shop, organizing my small stuff. I actually enjoy sorting through nails, bits and staples; and a pile of differently sized screws all thrown together drives me crazy. For this reason, I have become fond of Plano's plastic utility boxes. I have about 100 of them.

This might seem excessive, but I also use the boxes to organize and store fishing lures. In fact, these boxes often are advertised as miniature tackle boxes.

Any woodworker or angler knows that the amount of screws, nails, bits and lures one owns tends to grow exponentially, resulting in a lot of little stuff. (After sorting through my fishing lures recently I realized I own almost a thousand.) Plano's boxes have dividers to keep everything organized and they're easy to carry around the shop, to a job site or on a boat. However, 100 loose boxes is a bit like a pile of differently sized screws. I needed a box to organize my boxes. The cabinet you see here is the result.

This project is simple and quick to build – as a shop project should be. The plastic boxes merely slide in and out on pieces of Masonite that are slipped into dados cut on the inside of each side piece and both sides of the cabinet's center divider. The cope-and-stick doors are entirely optional.

While any miniature tackle box will work, this cabinet fits Plano's 3700-series utility boxes.

Rows of Dados

Cut the poplar top, bottom, sides, divider, plywood back and Masonite shelves to size, as stated in the cutting list. Now it's time to cut the dados. Install your dado stack in your table saw. Since the dados are ¼" wide by ¼" deep, you won't need to use a lot of shims or chippers from your dado set.

I spaced my dados 2¼" apart. You need to cut each dado on the inside of each side piece and on both sides of the center divider. Cut the first dado in the four places required, adjust your fence and

Cutting the dados is simple work with a dado set installed in your table saw. Cut four dados (one on each side piece and two on the divider), move the fence, then cut four more and so on.

Some heavy-duty screws will ensure this cabinet will stay put, even when fully stocked.

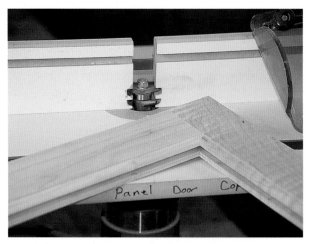

Two screw strips, one on the top and one on the bottom, allow you to screw your cabinet to your shop wall. Notice the notch cut into the divider to allow the screw strip to fit.

I built my cope-and-stick doors using a stile-and-rail bit set in my router. The doors are optional and can be made however you wish.

then cut the next one. You're cutting 11 dados on each face, which amounts to 44 dados. This method ensures you move your fence as little as possible.

With the dados complete, cut a ¼" x ¼" rabbet on the rear edge of the side pieces that will hold the ¼"-thick plywood back.

Assembling the Cabinet

Once the dados are cut, round over the edges of the top and bottom pieces using your router and a ½"-radius roundover bit. Sand all the case pieces to #180-grit.

Lay out where the sides and divider will go on the top and bottom, as shown in the illustration at right. Use these layout lines to drill your clearance holes, then screw the sides, top and bottom (but not the divider) together with #8 x 2" screws.

You need two screw strips to hang the cabinet on the wall – one on the top and one on the bottom, as shown in the drawing. While the screw strips fit between each side piece, you must first notch the center divider to make it work. Using your band saw, cut a ¾"-wide by 1½"-long notch at the top and bottom of the back side of the divider. Screw the divider in place and then nail the screw strips in place as well, as shown at left.

If you did everything correctly, the ¼"-thick plywood back should fit snugly between each side piece and flat against each screw strip. Basically, it fits into a ¼"-deep rabbet you created when assembling the cabinet. Cut your back to size, sand it smooth and, using your brad nailer, nail it in place.

Cope-and-stick Doors

The doors are optional. In a shop, they'll keep the boxes from getting dusty. Plus, they show off your craftsmanship. If and how you make them is up to you.

I made my two doors using stile-and-rail cutters on my router table. I used my table saw to raise the panel. First, cut all your door parts to size. Then, using your rail bit (sometimes called the cope-cutting bit), cut the tenon on the four rails. Then cut the beaded moulding profile and groove on your four stiles with the stile bit from your stile-and-rail bit set.

It's always a good idea to do test cuts when using stile-and-rail bits.

To raise the panel, head to your table saw and bevel the blade to 7°. Adjust the rip fence to leave a shoulder on the panel at the top of the blade and a thin-enough edge to fit into the grooves you just cut in your stiles and rails. Again, cutting a test piece first is a good idea to ensure a snug fit.

Supplies

Plano • planomolding.com or 800-226-9868
plastic utility boxes 3700 series, price varies
Rockler • rockler.com or 800-279-4441
4 partial wrap-around hinges #31495, $8.99/pair
2 narrow magnetic catches #26559, $2.49/each
2 classic wooden knobs #15257, $7.99/pair
Prices correct at time of publication.

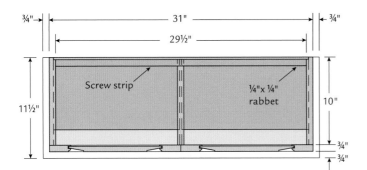

¾" ⊢——————— 31" ——————→ ⊣ ¾"

⊢———————— 29½" ————————→

Screw strip

¼" x ¼" rabbet

11½"

10"

¾"

¾"

PLAN - TOP REMOVED

Practical Shop Cabinet

NO.	ITEM	DIMENSIONS (INCHES)			MATERIAL
		T	**W**	**L**	
1	Top	¾	11½	32½	Poplar
1	Bottom	¾	11½	32½	Poplar
2	Sides	¾	10	30	Poplar
1	Divider	¾	9¾	30	Poplar
1	Back	¼	30	30	Plywood
22	Shelves	¼	8	14¹³⁄₁₆	Masonite
2	Screw strips	¾	1½	29½	Poplar
4	Door stiles	¾	2½	30	Poplar
4	Door rails	¾	2½	11¼*	Poplar
2	Door panels	¾	11⅛*	25¹¹⁄₁₆*	Poplar

*Finished size will vary depending on your set of rail-and-stile bits.

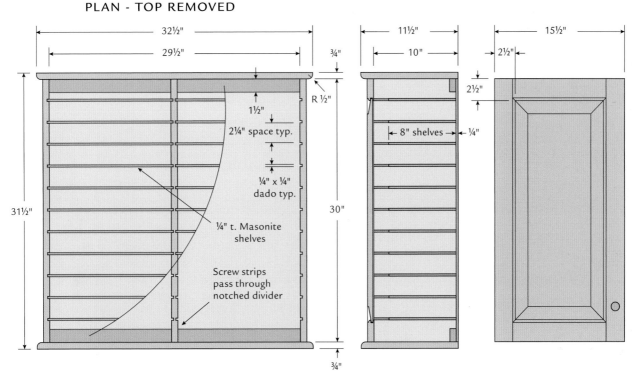

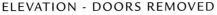

⊢——————— 32½" ——————→

⊢———————— 29½" ————————→

¾"

R ½"

1½"

2¼" space typ.

¼" x ¼" dado typ.

¼" t. Masonite shelves

Screw strips pass through notched divider

31½"

30"

¾"

ELEVATION - DOORS REMOVED

⊢— 11½" —→

⊢— 10" —→

2½"

2½"

15½"

8" shelves ← ¼"

SECTION   **DOOR ELEVATION**

Sand the panels to #180-grit before gluing them up in the frame-and-panel assemblies. Don't sand the inside edges of the rail-and-stile pieces at the point where they mate to form the joints. You could easily create an ugly gap.

Glue up the door assemblies. It's a loose-panel assembly, so don't glue the frames' grooves. As the seasons change, you want your panel to expand and contract.

I used four partial wrap-around hinges to attach the doors to the cabinet and two magnetic catches to keep them shut. Don't forget the wooden knobs.

Initially I painted my cabinet yellow, which is the color shown here. But I decided I didn't like the yellow, so later I painted it

black and then distressed the finish. There's no need to finish the Masonite shelves. Simply cut them to finished size and slide them into place.

This cabinet is the perfect solution for my woodworking and fishing storage needs. Whenever people visit my shop they comment on its ingenuity. It's so simple! There's only one problem: I didn't build this cabinet big enough. I'm currently working on a chimney cabinet design to resolve this issue.

Arts & Crafts Tool Cabinet

by Christopher Schwarz

Sometime while sawing the 60th dovetail for a drawer side, when my patience was as thin as the veneer facing on cheap plywood, a familiar feeling crept into my body. I began to experience an understandable lust for my biscuit joiner.

It sat patiently on a shelf, and I knew that its chattering, rattling teeth would make everything about this tool cabinet go much faster. But I resisted, because I had the words of a Victorian social reformer, art critic and part-time madman ringing in my head.

The writings of Englishman John Ruskin (1819-1900) were a cornerstone of the American Arts & Crafts movement. Ruskin decried the worst parts of 19th century industrialism. He promoted craft, pensions and public education when there was little of those things for the poor.

And in his book the "Seven Lamps of Architecture, The Lamp of Memory," which was published in 1849, he wrote a passage that all woodworkers should read. It's a bit long and a bit dramatic, but it has stuck with me just the same.

"When we build, let us think that we build forever. Let it not be for present delight nor for present use alone. Let it be such work as our descendants will thank us for; and let us think, as we lay stone on stone, that a time is to come when those stones will be held sacred because our hands have touched them, and that men will say, as they look upon the labor and wrought substance on them, 'See! This our father did for us.'"

The biscuit joiner stayed on the shelf. I continued to saw, chop, pare and fit for another four or five hours. Ruskin, I hoped, would have approved.

From the Book of Tolpin

While Ruskin kept me going through this long and difficult project, I really have a 20th century craftsman and author to thank (or blame) for my obsession with building a fine tool cabinet. Since it was first published in 1995, "The Toolbox Book" (Taunton Press) by Jim Tolpin has become the most-thumbed book in my library. I've studied every page, toolbox and drawing between its maroon cover boards (the dust jacket is long gone).

Years ago, I resolved to build myself a cabinet that might rival some of the examples in "The Toolbox Book." This year, I gave it my best shot. Since early 2004 I've spent many spare moments doodling on graph paper and on my computer to come up with a design that satisfied the three things I wanted from a cabinet: It had to hold a lot of tools, look good and be built to last. After studying my work habits, measuring all my tools and paging through thousands of examples of Arts & Crafts casework, this is what I came up with.

It's small but spacious. Have you ever ridden in an old Volkswagen Beetle? They are surprisingly roomy, and especially generous with the headroom. Somehow, the Beetle violates the laws of space and physics, and it is roomy but can also be parked between two oversized Hummers. This cabinet is designed to function the same way. The interior is a mere 11¼" deep, 22½" wide and 31½" tall. Yet, thanks to good planning, it holds every hand tool I need.

The cubbyholes and shelf for handplanes are carefully sized for all the planes needed in a modern shop. The drawers are loaded with trays of tools. Each tray contains all the tools for a routine function, such as dovetailing, sharpening or shaping curved surfaces.

The cabinet looks pretty good. I spent months thumbing through old Art & Crafts furniture catalogs and contemporary hardware catalogs for inspiration. This cabinet and its lines are a little bit Gustav Stickley, a little Harvey Ellis and a little of myself.

The cabinet will endure. No compromises were made in selecting the joints. Every major component (with the exception of the changeable, nailed-together trays) are built to withstand heavy use. Of course, when you discuss durable joints, you are usually talking dovetails, which is where we'll begin construction.

When sawing the tails, clamp the two sides together and cut them at the same time. This saves time and effort and prevents layout errors.

If your rabbets for the back are perfectly square, your case is much more likely to end up square, too. Clean up any imperfections with a rabbeting plane, such as this bullnose rabbet plane.

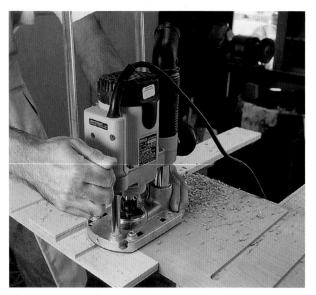

The shop-made T-square jig and a plunge router make quick work of the dados.

Here you can see how you use the dado cut into the jig to line up the jig with your layout lines. Using a router with a flat side on its base is more accurate than using a router with a round base.

A Case that Takes a Beating

When this cabinet is fully loaded, my best guess is that it weighs more than any single member of our staff at the magazine (modesty prevents me from revealing what that upper limit might be). To ensure the bottom and top pieces can withstand this weight, I joined them to the side pieces with through-dovetails.

One interesting variation worth noting here is that instead of using one solid top piece, I substituted two 3"-wide rails and dovetailed them into the sides to save a little weight. Because I cut these dovetails by hand, it was simple to lay out this unusual arrangement. If you plan to use a dovetail jig, you will save yourself a headache by forgetting the rails and making your top one solid piece instead.

If you're cutting the dovetails by hand, it's faster and more accurate to clamp your two sides together and saw the tails on the side pieces simultaneously. For years I resisted this technique because it seemed more difficult, but now I know better.

A second feature of the case to note is that the rabbet for the back is a hefty 1" wide. This allows room for the ½"-thick shiplapped back, plus a ½"-thick French cleat that will park the cabinet on the wall and keep it there.

And then there are the stopped dados. These ¼"-deep joints in the side pieces hold all the dividers. Cutting these joints is simple work with three tools: a plunge router, a bearing-guided straight bit and a shop-made T-square jig that guides the whole shebang. Lay out all the locations of your dados on the sides. Park the jig so it lines up with your layout lines. Cut the dados in two passes.

Fitting all the horizontal dividers to fit the dados is easy. The ½"-thick dividers simply need a small notch at the front to fit over the rounded end of the dado created by the round straight bit. A sharp backsaw is just the tool here.

Fitting the dividers is easy with a handplane. I merely make sure the dividers are surfaced a few thousandths of an inch thicker than where I want them to be. Then I thin them down with a smoothing plane until they slide in with just a little persuasion.

The ¾"-thick horizontal divider needs a bit more work to fit in the ½"-wide dado. A ¼" x ¼" end-rabbet is the answer.

The through-dados that hold the vertical dividers use the same router jig, but with the plunge router set to make only an ⅛"-deep cut. Laying out the locations of these parts for the handplane cubbyholes might seem daunting. If you want the openings evenly spaced, they should each be 3.333" wide. I don't have any infinite numbers on my ruler. But it's actually child's play to lay out the cubbyholes with a pair of dividers (they look like a school compass but with two pointy tips — no pencil). You can tweak these tools until they step off the cubbyholes as precisely as you please. Dividers are one of my secret weapons.

With all these parts cut and fit, make the back of the case. I used ambrosia maple. It's cheap and looks a bit like the spalted maple I used in the doors and drawers. The back boards are joined by a ¼"-deep x ⅜"-wide shiplap on each long edge.

After gluing the sides to the bottom and top rails, trim the dovetails flush with a block plane. Soak the end grain with a little bit of mineral spirits to make it easier to cut. Here you can also see how I supported the case as I worked on it. The big slab holding up the side is an offcut from an old door that's clamped to my bench.

Cut the rabbet on the backside of the door using a rabbeting bit in your router table. With a large tabletop such as this, it's simple work.

The top cap is easy. Cut the wide chamfer on the underside using your table saw. Clean up the cut with a block plane. Attach the top to the rails with screws.

You are now at a critical juncture. You can go ahead and get some quick gratification and assemble the whole case. But good luck when you go to finish it. Getting those cubbyholes finished right will be murder. The better solution is to glue up only the sides, bottom and top rails. Tape off the exposed joints and finish all the case parts (I used two coats of a satin spray lacquer). Then assemble the case. I know it sounds like a pain (it is). But the end result is worth it.

Finish the back pieces and top cap while you're at it. Now you can screw the back in place and the top cap. You are ready for the doors and drawers.

Easier than They Look

The doors aren't too bad. The mullions and muntins that form the four lights in each door appear difficult, but thanks to a little legerdemain, it's no problem.

But before getting mired in those details, you need to assemble the doors. Here's how they work: The stiles and rails are joined using mortise-and-tenon joints. For mid-size doors such as these, I use ⅜"-thick x 1"-long tenons.

Cut your tenons and your mortises, then mill a ¼"-wide x ⅜"-deep groove in the rails and stiles to hold the door panel. I generally make this groove on the router table using a straight bit and featherboards. It's the easiest way to make the groove start and stop in the right place in the stiles.

The door panel needs a rabbet on its back to fit in the groove. But before you mill the panel, you should know a bit about spalted maple. Its black spidery lines are caused by the spalt fungus, which attacks the tree after it's been felled. In short, it's partly rotted.

It's always best to wear a respirator when dealing with spalted wood. There are numerous accounts of people who have had respiratory problems after breathing in the dust.

Once you fit the panel, assemble the doors – the mullions and muntins are added after assembly. Once the glue cures, cut a ¼"-wide x ½"-deep rabbet on the backside of the opening for the glass.

Glue one backing strip into the rabbet in the door on edge. Then flip the door over and glue a mullion onto the backing strip. Then use spring clamps to hold everything while the glue dries.

Install the horizontal muntins the same way. First glue a backing strip into the rabbet on the backside of the door. Then flip the door over and glue the muntin to that.

This rabbet will hold the narrow backing strips that are built up into the mullions and muntins.

This technique was explained fully by Glen Huey in our August 2002 issue ("Simple Divided-light Glass Doors"). But the photos above explain it better than words can. Essentially, you create the T-shaped moulding that makes the mullions and muntins by gluing together ¼"-thick x ½"-wide strips of wood. It's simple work.

What's not so simple is mounting the doors with the strap hinges. These hinges are inexpensive, beautiful and handmade. As a result, they need a bit of tweaking and bending and hammering and cursing to get them just right to hang a door.

Here's my best tip: Screw the hinges in place with the cabinet on its back. Then stand it up, loosen the hinge screws and make your final adjustments. I used a block plane to make some adjustments, and a mallet for others. Let your frustration level be your guide.

Getting a Handle on Drawers

The drawers are a long slog. Even though I'm a fair dovetailer, it took me three solid days of work to get the drawers assembled and fit. But before you start listening to that lock-miter router bit whispering in your ear, remember this: The drawers are going to hold

Arts & Crafts Tool Cabinet

NO.	ITEM	DIMENSIONS (INCHES)			MATERIAL	COMMENTS
		T	W	L		
Carcase						
2	Sides	¾	12¼	33	Cherry	⅜"-deep x 1"-wide rabbet at back
2	Top rails	¾	3	24	Cherry	Dovetailed into sides
1	Bottom	¾	11¼	24	Cherry	Dovetailed into sides
1	Top cap	1	17	32	Cherry	½"-deep x 3"-wide bevel
	Shiplapped back	½	23¼	33	Maple	¼" x ¼" shiplaps
1	Major horizontal divider	¾	10½	23	Cherry	In ¼"-deep x ½"-wide dados
1	Thin horizontal divider	½	10½	23	Cherry	In ¼"-deep x ½"-wide dados
3	Thin horizontal dividers	½	9¼	23	Cherry	In ¼"-deep x ½"-wide dados
5	Vertical dividers	½	10	6½	Cherry	In ⅛"-deep x ½"-wide dados
2	Small vertical dividers	½	9¼	2¾	Cherry	In ⅛"-deep x ½"-wide dados
Doors						
2	Large stiles	¾	2¾	33	Cherry	
2	Small stiles	¾	1¼	33	Cherry	
2	Top rails	¾	2¾	10	Cherry	1" TBE
2	Intermediate rails	¾	2¼	10	Cherry	1" TBE
2	Lower rails	¾	3¾	10	Cherry	1" TBE
2	Panels	½	8½	16¾	Maple	In ¼"-wide x ⅜"-deep groove
2	Vertical muntins	¼	½	8	Cherry	
4	Horizontal muntins	¼	½	3¾	Cherry	
2	Backing strips	¼	½	8½	Cherry	In ¼"-wide x ½"-deep rabbet, glued to vertical muntin
4	Small backing strips	¼	½	4⅛	Cherry	Glued to horizontal muntin
Drawers						
4	Small drawer fronts	¾*	2½	11	Maple	¼"-deep x ½" rabbet on bottom edge
8	Small drawer sides	½	2½	9	Poplar	¼"-deep x ¼" rabbet on bottom edge
4	Small drawer backs	½	2¼	11	Poplar	
4	Small drawer bottoms	¼	10½	9	Plywood	Screwed to drawer box
1	Medium drawer front	¾*	5	22½	Maple	¼"-deep x ¼"-wide groove for bottom
2	Medium drawer sides	½	5	9	Poplar	¼"-deep x ¼"-wide groove for bottom
1	Medium drawer back	½	4½	22½	Poplar	
1	Medium drawer bottom	½	8¾	22	Plywood	¼"-deep x ½" rabbet on bottom edge
1	Large drawer front	¾*	6¾	22½	Maple	¼"-deep x ¼"-wide groove for bottom
2	Large drawer sides	½	6¾	9	Poplar	¼"-deep x ¼"-wide groove for bottom
1	Large drawer back	½	6½	22½	Poplar	
1	Large drawer bottom	½	8¾	22	Plywood	¼"-deep x ½" rabbet on bottom edge

* Finished dimension, laminated from two pieces of wood; TBE= tenon, both ends

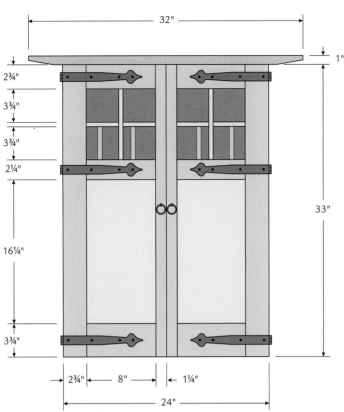

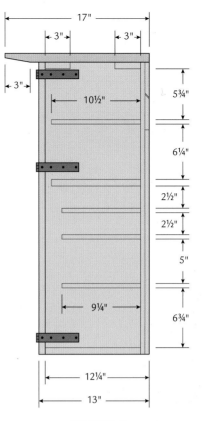

ELEVATION – DOORS CLOSED

PROFILE

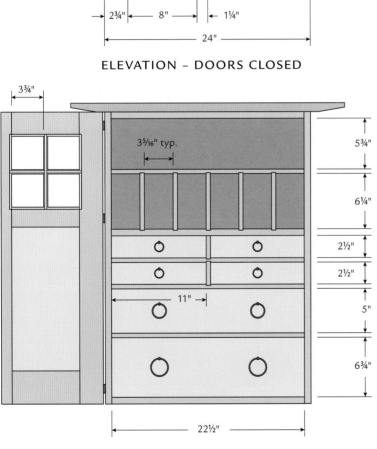

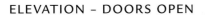

ELEVATION – DOORS OPEN

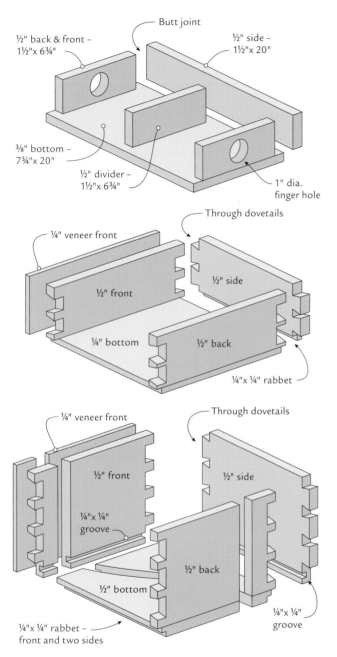

½" back & front –
1½" x 6¾"

Butt joint

½" side –
1½" x 20"

⅜" bottom –
7¾" x 20"

½" divider –
1½" x 6¾"

1" dia.
finger hole

¼" veneer front

Through dovetails

½" front

½" side

¼" bottom

½" back

¼" x ¼" rabbet

¼" veneer front

Through dovetails

½" front

½" side

¼" x ¼"
groove

½" back

½" bottom

¼" x ¼" rabbet –
front and two sides

¼" x ¼"
groove

LARGE DRAWER JOINERY

Build the drawers with through-dovetails. Then glue a piece of ¼"-thick veneer to the front.

Here you can see the two different ways of installing the drawer bottoms. The bottom in the top drawer rests in a rabbet in the sides. The drawer bottom for the larger drawers slides into a groove.

Install the dividers in the drawers so they can be easily removed in the future. A 23-gauge pinner is an excellent tool for this job.

Once everything is finished, install the glass using small strips of cherry (⅛" and ¼" thick). A few dabs of clear silicone and a couple small pins do the trick.

a tremendous amount of steel. And when you open the drawers during a future project, you'll never be disappointed to see dovetails.

To make things a tad easier, I built all the drawers using through-dovetails and ½"-thick material for the front, sides and back. Then, with the drawer glued up, I glued on a ¼"-thick piece of spalted maple to the front piece. This trick also allowed me to stretch my supply of spalted maple.

The four small drawers are built a little differently than the two larger ones. Because the small drawers are shallow, I wanted to use every bit of space. So the bottom is ¼"-thick plywood that's nailed into a ¼" x ¼" rabbet on the drawer's underside.

The larger drawers are more conventional. Plow a ¼" x ¼" groove in the sides and front pieces to hold a ½"-thick bottom, which is rabbeted to fit in the groove.

Build all the drawers to fit their openings exactly, then use a jack plane to shave the sides until the drawer slides like a piston. Finish the doors and drawers, then it's time for the fun part: dividing up the drawers, building trays for the tools and tweaking the hardware so everything works just right.

As you divide up the drawers and trays, one word of advice: Don't fasten any of the dividers permanently. Your tool set will change, and you want to be able to easily alter the dividers. I fit mine in place with friction and a couple 23-gauge headless pins. The dividers can be wrenched free when I need room for a new tool.

When you hang the cabinet, use wide cleats – mine were each 5" wide. This allows you to get more screws into the cabinet and into the studs. Also, for extra insurance, I rested the bottom of the cabinet on a 2"-wide ledger that also was screwed into the studs.

With the project complete, the voice of Ruskin was finally silenced for a short time as I assessed my work. (I for one was happy

for the silence; Ruskin vacillated between madness and lucidity during the last years of his life.) I scolded myself for a few things: the reveals around the drawers on the left edge of the cabinet are a tad wider than the reveals on the right side. And in a couple of the dovetails at the rear of the drawers, there are a couple small gaps. It's not perfect.

But before I got too down on myself, I remembered one more quote from Ruskin that relates to handwork and the pursuit of perfection. This one deserves as much ink as the first.

"No good work whatever can be perfect," he writes, "and the demand for perfection is always a sign of a misunderstanding of the ends of art."

Supplies

Lee Valley Tools • leevalley.com or 800-871-8158

6 28mm ring pulls, 01A61.28, $3 each
2 40mm ring pulls, 01A61.40, $4.50 each
2 50mm ring pulls, 01A61.50, $5.30 each
6 Unequal strap hinges, 9½ " x 3½", 01H21.33, $11.40 each
4 Magnetic catches, 00S16.01, $1.70 each
7 #6 x ⅝" black pyramid-head screws (bags of 10), 01X38.65,
   $1.40 a bag
Prices as of publication date.

Traveling Tool Chest

by Christopher Schwarz

Since I started woodworking in about 1993, I've stored my tools in almost every way imaginable – from plastic buckets to wall cabinets, racks and a variety of tool chests.

After exploring each of these methods, I kept coming back to a traditional tool chest because I have not found a better way to protect and organize my tools. I also appreciate the finite capacity of a tool chest – it forces me to think hard before buying an additional tool.

During most visits to the tool store I conclude: If it doesn't fit in the chest, I probably don't need it.

The Right Chest Size

Tool chests are built in a number of fairly standard sizes that are based on the sizes of typical tools and the limits of our bodies.

Large floor chests are usually about 24" x 24" x 40" and are designed to hold full-size saws and large jointer planes, which can be longer than 30". These chests also hold a full set of moulding planes, bench planes and all the small tools needed to make any piece of furniture. These chests are difficult to move alone, which is a disadvantage if you are by yourself, but is an advantage if someone is trying to steal your chest (the thief needs an accomplice).

Medium-size chests are just big enough to hold panel saws and smaller metal jointer planes – about 18" x 18" x 30" – and can be picked up by one person. It's an ideal size for someone who works alone, has to move the chest on occasion and doesn't require a full set of moulding planes.

This medium-size chest can hold a remarkable amount of tools – two panel saws, three backsaws, the three standard bench planes, a rabbet plane, plow and router plane all fit on its floor. The two sliding trays and rack hold everything else you (should) need.

Smaller chests – the third size – were usually used for site work or by "gentlemen" woodworkers who had a small kit of tools.

The medium-size chest in this chapter is ideal for someone getting started in woodworking with a small shop and a budding kit

of tools. It's easy to build, fairly tough and can easily be transported to schools. When I build tool chests for customers, this is far and away the most requested size.

How It's Built

The carcase is dovetailed together – the strongest joint available. The bottom boards are, however, nailed onto the carcase so they are easily replaced if they rot. Speaking of rot, the entire chest sits on two oak "rot strips" screwed to the bottom boards, keeping the chest off a wet floor.

The bottom and top skirts on this chest are mitered and nailed to the carcase. I typically dovetail the skirts at the corners, but a well-made miter can survive just fine.

The lid is a thick panel that is surrounded by a dust seal on three sides; the seal pieces are dovetailed at the corners because this area of a tool chest takes heaps of abuse.

THE GANG'S ALL HERE. When cutting through-dovetails, I gang-cut the tail boards to save time and effort.

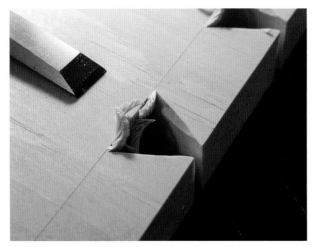

EASE THE ENTRY. Beveling the interior corners of the tail boards makes assembly easier. And you are much less likely to damage your tails when driving them into the pins.

Most of the carcase is made from a lightweight and inexpensive wood such as pine. The parts that will see heavy wear are oak. We'll discuss the interior fittings after we get the carcase complete.

Make the Shell

Join the corners of the carcase with through-dovetails – six dovetails at each corner are suitable for a chest this size. Smooth the inside faces of the boards and assemble the carcase. Once the glue is dry, level the joints and remove the tool marks from the case's exterior.

Now fetch the pine bottom boards. The grain should run from front to back in the chest (for strength), and the long edges of the boards should have some sort of joint to accommodate wood movement. I used the tongue-and-groove joint. Then I cut a 3/16" bead on the tongue boards as decoration.

Attach the bottom boards to the carcase with 6d headed nails – I used cut clouts. Be sure to leave some room between the boards

LONG SLEEVES. Sleeve the assembled carcase over your benchtop to make it easy to level the front and back of the chest.

GROOVE YOUR BOTTOM, THEN TONGUE IT. I use a tongue-and-groove plane to cut the joints on the long edges of the bottom boards. This plane cuts both the male and female bits.

TWEAKED. If your carcase isn't square, clamp across the long diagonal to pull it square while you nail on the bottom boards.

RESIST ROT. Either make your rot strips impervious to water (plastic would work, too), or make them so they will rot off immediately by using pine and iron nails. Either way works.

for expansion and contraction. Trim the bottom boards flush with the carcase.

The last bit on the shell is to attach the rot strips to the underside of the bottom boards. I use water-resistant white oak and attach it to the bottom with waterproof glue and brass screws. After finishing, I oil and wax these rot strips to make them repel water.

Mitered Skirting

The bottom skirt protects the carcase from kicks and bumps. The top skirt helps seal the interior from dust and protects the lid's dust seal. The skirting is ½"-thick stuff that wraps around the entire carcase and is mitered at the corners.

Before cutting the miters, however, cut any moulding or bevels. These are not just decorative – a 90° corner is fragile and will quickly splinter off in the shop. I used a ⅜" square ovolo on the bottom skirt. The top skirt has a ⅛" bead on its top edge and a 30° bevel on the bottom edge.

Now attach the skirting to the carcase. I miter moulding with a miter box, which I find more accurate than power equipment. All the miters here were assembled right from the saw. That's not

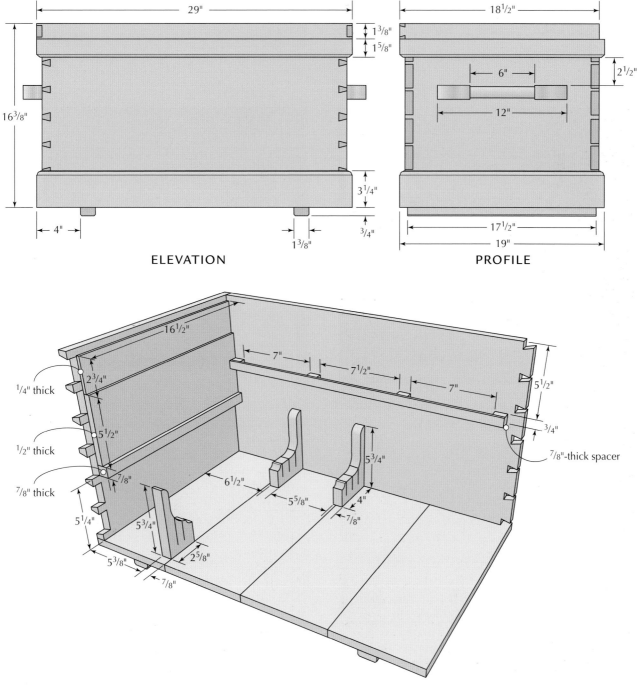

ELEVATION

PROFILE

INTERIOR FITTINGS

COMPLETELY STUCK. Mould the entire stick of wood before cutting it apart for mitering. This ensures the moulding will match at the corners.

MITERS ALL AROUND. I begin mitering at one front corner of the chest. I get that joint perfect, then I make my way around the carcase.

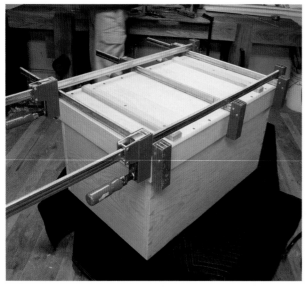

YES, CLAMP. Glue the short grain of each miter and clamp it at the corners. The glue will have more strength this way.

THIS HIGH. The 5¼"-wide spacer acts as a shelf when installing the runner above it. The 5¼" height is critical for holding standard bench planes below the bottom tray.

because I'm awesome; it's because a miter box allows you to put a sawtooth right on a knife line.

Glue and nail the skirting to the carcase – don't forget to apply glue to the miters themselves. Then clamp the corners while the glue dries. At this point I fitted out the interior with trays, saw tills and a rack.

The Interior

The arrangement shown in this chest is typical and works well. On the floor of the chest are two small saw tills – one for backsaws and the other for two panel saws. I like these tills because they take up little space.

Floating above the floor are two sliding trays – one deep and one shallow. The deep tray is for bulky tools such as the brace and bit, plus anything in a tool roll. The top tray is for all the small tools you use every day – layout tools, a block plane, a mallet, hammer and wax, for example.

The walls of the trays are made from pine. The bottoms and the runners they slide on are made from oak to resist wear.

On the back wall of the chest is a simple rack for holding chisels and other small or handled tools – dividers, combination squares and screwdrivers.

Install the Runners

The sliding trays run on oak runners that are affixed to the inside of the carcase. There are three layers of runners for the two trays, all of different thicknesses and widths so that the trays can be pulled up and out of the carcase.

The lowest runners are installed 5¼" from the floor of the chest – that gives your bench planes the headroom they need. I install these lower runners by first making a spacer board from

Traveling Tool Chest

NO.	ITEM	T	W	L	MATERIAL
			DIMENSIONS (INCHES)		
2	Front/back	¾	14⅞	28	Pine
2	Ends	¾	14⅞	18	Pine
1	Bottom*	⅝	28	18	Pine
2	Rot strips	¾	1⅜	17½	Oak
2	Bottom skirt, front/back	½	3¼	29	Pine
2	Bottom skirt, ends	½	3¼	19	Pine
2	Top skirt, front/back	½	1⅝	29	Pine
2	Top skirt, ends	½	1⅝	19	Pine
2	Chest lifts	1¼	1¾	12	Oak
1	Lid panel	⅞	18¹⁄₁₆	28⅜	Pine**
1	Dust seal, front	½	1½	29	Pine
2	Dust seal, ends	½	1½	19	Pine
Interior Fittings					
2	Bottom runners	⅞	⅞	16½	Oak
2	Middle runners	½	5½	16½	Oak
2	Top runners	¼	2¾	16½	Oak
Bottom Tray					
2	Front/back	½	5⅛	25⅜	Pine
2	Ends	½	5⅛	8	Pine
1	Bottom	¼	8	25½	Oak
Top Tray					
2	Front/back	½	2½	25⅞	Pine
2	Ends	½	2½	8	Pine
1	Bottom	¼	8	26	Oak
Tool holders					
1	Panel-saw till	⅞	2⅝	5¾	Oak
2	Backsaw tills	⅞	4	5¾	Oak
1	Rack, front piece	¼	¾	25½	Oak
4	Rack spacers	⅝	¾	1	Oak

*Made from multiple boards; **Plywood if making a marquetry lid.

Supplies

Tremont Nail Co.
tremontnail.com or 800-835-0121
6d clout nails, #CT6, $13.09
(1 lb. box)
Peter Ross, Blacksmith
peterrossblacksmith.com,
919-663-3309 or
rosspm@msn.com
2 Chest hinges
1 Crab lock
Call for pricing.

SMOOTH-SLIDING BOTTOM. The bottom boards are the only part that touches the runners. So shoot them to perfect length until you get the sliding action you want with zero racking.

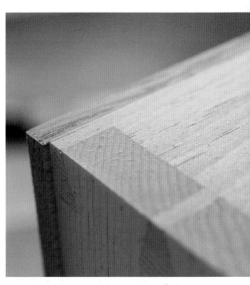

PROUD BOTTOM. Here you can see how the bottom protrudes from the end of the tray, making the tray a cinch to fit.

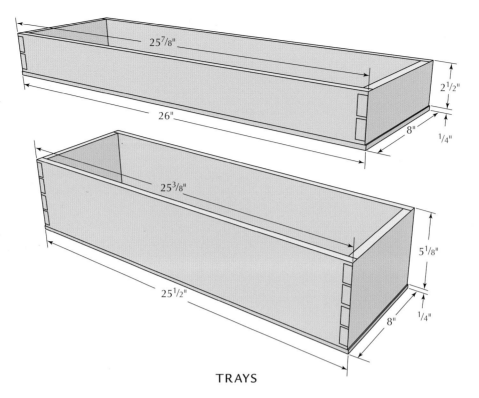

TRAYS

some scrap that is 5¼" wide (see photo on page 130). I use that as a temporary shelf to hold the lower runners in position while I glue and nail them.

After the lower runners are installed, remove the spacer and install the runners above, also with nails and glue. I cut a small bead on the top edge of each to protect the corner from damage and to spruce up the interior a bit.

Build the Trays

The trays are dovetailed at the corners and each has a thin oak bottom that is nailed on. The interesting detail here is that the finished trays are ⅛" smaller than the bottoms are long. In other words, the bottoms are ¹⁄₁₆" proud on either end of the assembled trays.

This detail makes the trays easy to fit. You only have to get the bottoms to slide smoothly on the runners. The trays never touch the runners or interfere with the sliding action.

So fit the bottom boards so they are a close but smooth fit on the runners.

Now dovetail and assemble the trays. Then nail or screw the bottoms on. If you need to use multiple boards for the bottoms, shiplap the joints at their mating edges.

Racks & Tills

I like simple racks and tills for my chests because that leaves more room to arrange the tools. The rack on the back wall is made from scrap bits of oak that I glued together, then screwed onto the back wall with No. 8 x 1¼" screws.

The saw till for the panel saws is simply one piece of oak with two kerfs cut into it. One kerf is for the crosscut saw and the second for the rip saw. This till holds the saws at their tips. The weight of

RACK AT THE BACK. This simple rack can hold a variety of tools. My other favorite form of rack is a board that is poked with ½"-diameter holes on 1⅛" centers.

QUICK SAW TILL. Kerf the block of wood for the saws, then shape the block so it looks nice (above). Then screw it to the side of the carcase and to a bottom board (right).

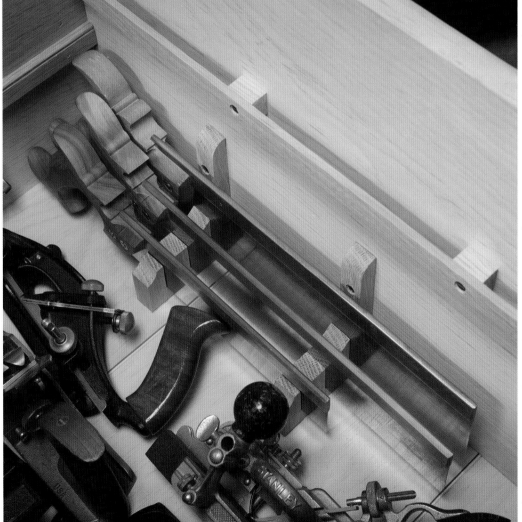

LOADING UP. The backsaw till offers more protection than the panel-saw till because backsaws are more fragile.

TURN THE BONE. The center section of the dog bone is turned down to 1" diameter. Then remove the piece from the lathe.

RASP THE BONE. Then shape the ends of the lifts. This shape leaves plenty of meat for the screws to bite into.

SCREWED EITHER WAY. Affix the lifts with stout #8 screws from both the inside and outside of the carcase.

the handle and the teeth at the heel of the saw prevents the tools from whipping around in the chest.

The till for the backsaws is made and attached in the same manner. The only difference is that there are two blocks of wood and three kerfs in each for the dovetail, carcase and tenon saw. This till is at the back of the chest.

Chest Lifts

While you should carry your chest by holding its bottom (or put it on a cart), the lifts help you get the chest into position or to balance your load. Each lift is made from a single piece of oak that looks like a dog's bone when you begin. You turn down the center to make a handle. Then shape the ends of the "bone" to make them look nice. I used a simple ogee curve.

The proper way to attach the lifts is to screw them in place from both the outside and the inside of the chest. The screws from the outside pass through the narrow ends of the lifts. The screws from the inside are driven into the thick part near the handle.

The Lid

The lid on my chest has some very nice marquetry, which you can include if you have the time and inclination, but a plain interior is fine. *[Editor's note: The marquetry shown on this chest is covered in detail in the October 2015 issue of Popular Woodworking Magazine — available at shopwoodworking.com/popular-woodworking-magazine-october-2015-download.]* If you are skipping the marquetry panel, make the lid from a softwood that doesn't move much, such as one of the white pines. And glue it up from several pieces of quartersawn or rift-sawn stock to further reduce seasonal movement.

After cutting the panel to size — it's a bit larger than the rim of the carcase — attach it to the carcase with hinges. With the lid in its final position, you then can build the dust seal around it to create a perfect fit.

RABBET THE SEAL. The rabbet on this piece of the dust seal allows you to sneak up on the perfect fit all around.

RABBETED DOVE-TAILS. This joinery looks a little involved, but it's actually simple. Begin by cutting a tail on the seal, then show it to its mate. You'll then know what to do.

After building about 20 of these chests, I have found a better way to make the dust seal fit. I rabbet each piece until that piece fits perfectly flush with the top skirt and the top edge of the lid. I can adjust this fit in tiny increments with a shoulder plane.

Then, once all three pieces of the dust seal fit perfectly, I dovetail them together at the corners.

I attach the seal using a combination of glue and nails. Glue and nail the front edge of the dust seal to the lid. To attach the "returns" along the ends of the chest, use glue and nails along the front 4" of the lid. Then use nails alone for the rest. This fastening method allows the top to move.

To keep the chest secure, I installed a traditional crab lock – a blacksmith-made lock built for chests that allows for some wood movement. They are easy to install because they are surface-mounted to the inside of the chest. And they are gorgeous.

The Best Finish

Almost all traditional tool chests were painted. It is the most durable and easy-to-renew finish. You can use any paint you like – milk paint, oil paint or latex. Paint the outside of the chest, but leave the inside of the chest bare – or use a coat of wax alone if you like.

If you insist on a film finish for the inside, use shellac. Please avoid oils – they will stink forever.

Once your chest is complete, my final caution is to avoid bringing it into your house. Many chests like this begin their lives intending to hold tools but somehow end up at the foot of the bed stuffed with blankets and doilies. A sad situation, indeed.

KEYHOLED. The only tough part about installing a crab lock is cutting a well-placed and crisp keyhole. I bore the hole for the round part of the key. Then I cut the remainder with a chisel.

Chapter Twenty-One

Router Cabinet

by Glen D. Huey

As I look around my shop, or most woodworking shops, I see cabinets built with plywood and screws. But there are other options. I decided to change things up and make a shop cabinet using hardwoods, and to use the project to experiment with a couple of different techniques.

I consider a router an essential woodworking tool. And because I have router bits and accessories stored in small boxes, stuck in drawers and in tool boxes (and hanging in less-than-ideal locations), a cabinet for all things router seemed the perfect project.

Build the Frame

The first order of business is to select and mill wood for the sides, top, shelves and center divider. Cut the top and sides to size, but leave the shelves and center divider ¼" overwide and 1" overlong.

Dovetails are perfect to join the cabinet sides to the top; the joint – tails in the sides – holds up extremely well under the stress of heavy use and weight.

The dovetails are hidden by an applied moulding – and if I'm hiding the work, I don't wish to see any indication of the joinery. To pull off the disappearing act, cut ⅛"-deep rabbets on the inside face of the ends of the top. This reduces the apparent thickness of the

top as seen from the ends, but doesn't give up any actual meat. Plus, the small shoulder helps hold the cabinet square during assembly.

Lay out the pin board (the top) with a wide pin at the back. Make your saw cuts, remove the waste, then transfer the layout to the sides. Remember to set your marking gauge to match the remaining thickness on the top's end before scribing any lines. I use a band saw to define the tails, then clear away the waste with chisels and fit the dovetails. Because the joints are covered by moulding, they don't need to be perfect.

When the joints slip together, you can see the value of the rabbets and how they help to hold the cabinet square.

Position the sides on your bench with the insides up, rear edges touching. Mark the locations for all the shelves and the cabinet bottom. (All are ¾" thick, excepting the ⅝"-thick router bit shelves.) The tricky part is that the sides have different layouts. The left side has a 90° shelf and bottom and five router-bit shelves angled downward at 15°. The right-side layout is simply three ¾"-wide dados, laid out following the plan.

Now calculate and cut the center divider to width (leave it overlong) and the long shelf to length and width. The vertical divider nestles into ¼"-deep dados cut in the top and long shelf. Now's a great time to locate and mark the top and long shelf for those dados.

THINK AHEAD. A wide pin at the rear of the top provides a solid area into which the side rabbets terminate, without showing from the outside of the cabinet.

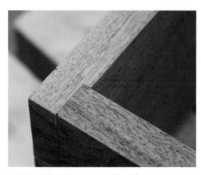

A WAY TO HIDE. A small rabbet cut into the ends of the cabinet top easily allows the joinery to be covered with full-thickness mouldings.

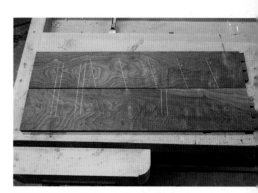

NOT IDENTICAL. The dados don't match in the cabinet sides. Work carefully as you mark the layout.

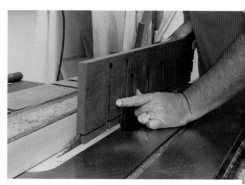

JIG NO. 1. A simple square platform jig in conjunction with a bearing-guided router bit makes quick work of the straight dados.

JIG NO. 2. A second simple jig – this one set at an angle, then reset in the opposite direction – knocks out the router-bit shelf dados.

NO STACK NEEDED. Cut rabbets in two quick steps at the table saw – first with the stick flat the table, then on edge.

Router Jigs Work Best

It's time to cut the ¼"-deep dados. I find two simple jigs are the best method of work. Each is built from scrap plywood and screwed together. The square platform jig is sized in thickness to work with a ¾" pattern bit. (My bit has a 1¼" cutting length, so if it's to cut a ¼"-deep dado, the jig has to be at least 1" thick.) Stack three pieces of ½" Baltic-birch ply, screw them together, then add a ½"-thick piece at one end to catch the workpiece and hold the jig square. (Fine-tune it as needed to bring the jig square to the workpiece.)

Align the jig to the left side of the cut and clamp it in position. A single clamp secures the jig. Rout the dado, allowing the bearing to ride against the jig. Stop your cuts about ½" from the front edge of the workpiece.

The angled dados are made the same way, except that the catch on the bottom of the jig is angled to match the layout. The router bit I used here is ⅝" in diameter; I set it up in a second router for more efficient work. Cut the angled dados into the cabinet side so the top edge of the dado is 4½" long.

Before moving on, cut rabbets for the back and rear support (the peg board). I used a ¾" wide x ⁷⁄₁₆"deep rabbet that I cut in two passes at the table-saw. I also cut a 1/4"-deep rabbet along

the back edge of the top to make sliding in the center divider easy. (This creates a slight gap at the sides, but it's covered by the moulding.)

Next, align the divider to the left side, then transfer the layout of the bit shelves. Mark both the top and bottom of the dados to account for the jig's placement – always to the left of the cut. Before routing the dados, the angle of the jig needs to be reversed. Remove its catch, position the jig to the new layout lines, then locate and re-attach the catch in its new position. Rout the dados as before.

Now rout 90° dados into the top and the long shelf for the vertical divider. (See why I set up two routers?)

Puzzle Comes Together

To fit the interior pieces of the cabinet, cut the shelves to length, then notch them to step out of the dados. I use a table saw for this. Set the fence for ¼" total cut (don't forget to account for the blade thickness), raise the blade to just more than ½", then, with a couple of quick passes, notch the ends.

Assemble the dovetail joints and slip the long shelf into position. With a couple of clamps holding things secure, fit the divider, making sure the angled dados align (small adjustments

EXACTING LAYOUT. The best way to mark for the opposing-angled dados for the center divider is directly off the cabinet side.

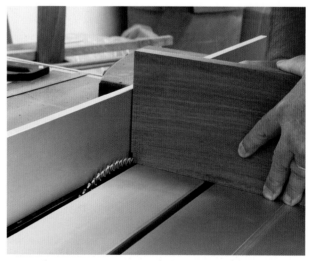

STEP OUT. Each of the parts housed in dados (except for the bit shelves) need to be notched at the ends; it's a simple and clean process using a table saw.

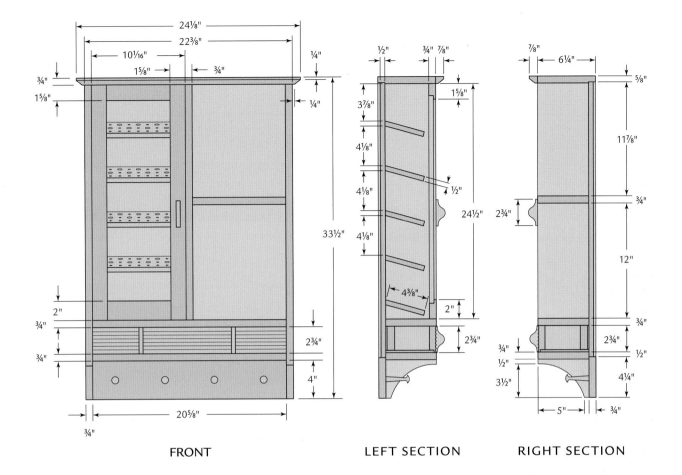

FRONT   **LEFT SECTION**   **RIGHT SECTION**

Router Cabinet

NO.	ITEM	DIMENSIONS (INCHES)			MATERIAL	COMMENTS
		T	W	L		
2	Sides	¾	6¼	33½	Walnut	
1	Top	¾	6¼	22⅜	Walnut	
1	Bottom	¾	5½	21⅜	Walnut	
1	Long shelf	¾	51½	21⅜	Walnut	
1	Vertical divider	¾	5½	25	Walnut	
1	Router shelf	¾	5½	10⁹⁄₁₆	Walnut	
5	Bit shelves	⅝	4⅜	10⁹⁄₁₆	Walnut	One edge angle cut*
1	Rear support	¾	4¼	21¾	Walnut	
1	Back	½	21¾	28⅝	Plywood	
2	Door stiles	¾	1⅝	24½	Walnut	
1	Upper door rail	¾	1⅝	9⁵⁄₁₆	Walnut	1¼" TBE**
1	Lower door rail	¾	2	9⁵⁄₁₆	Walnut	1¼" TBE**
1	Drawer front	¾	2¾	20⅞	Cherry	
1	Drawer back	½	2½	20⅜	Poplar	
2	Drawer sides	½	2½	5	Poplar	
1	Drawer bottom	¼	5½	20⅞	Poplar	
3	Pulls	⁷⁄₁₆	2¾	1	Walnut	
1	Crown moulding	¾	⅞	48	Walnut	
4	Pegs		½	3½	Walnut	

*Front and back edges are ripped at a 15° angle; **Tenon both ends

GET LEVEL. Small adjustments to get the angled shelves aligned makes it better to mark the single router shelf dado directly off the side location; measure, mark then rout.

ODD ARC. With the limited height of the arc, it's best to slip a scrap into position to more easily use your compass.

YOUR CHOICE. The top moulding is attached to the cabinet to cover the dovetail joints. Use your favorite profile.

are easily made). Notch the ends at the table saw, then slip the divider into position.

Next, mark the location of the router shelf on the divider. Measurements taken off the assembled cabinet better allow for level shelves. Cut the shelf to size and notch the ends before checking its fit. Repeat these steps to fit the bottom.

Now disassemble the cabinet and place the two sides inside up on your bench with the back edges matched. The last step is to lay out and cut the quarter-round design at the ends of the sides. The radius is 5"; the height is 3½". To facilitate using a compass for layout, slide a scrap along the bottom edge of the matched sides, then draw the half-circle as shown at top right. Make the cut, then smooth the edges.

Sand the insides and assemble the cabinet. The two flat shelves, divider and bottom are fit in their dados and secured using screws and plugs. (It's simple, but this is a shop cabinet.) Glue and assemble the dovetails. Position the long shelf, then drill and countersink for the screws, two at each end. Repeat the steps for the divider and router shelf.

If you want to plug the divider holes in the long shelf, do that prior to attaching the bottom. There's little room to work after that

shelf is installed. To wrap up assembly, fill the holes with plugs of matched grain, then after the glue dries, sand the surfaces smooth.

The cabinet is topped with a simple piece of moulding cut with one of my favorite ogee bits, a classic design. Attach the moulding using glue and pins. (Don't neglect to glue the miters.)

Now is the perfect time to add the rear support, which holds turned pegs. The support fits into the same rabbet you cut for the back. Two screws per end hold it in place. Lay out and drill for the pegs prior to installing the support.

Build the Door

Beginning woodworkers often build doors by joining the rails and stiles with mortise-and-tenon joints, then routing the back of the door using a rabbet bit. This results in a small section of exposed end grain at each corner. There is a better technique.

With just a couple of extra steps in the process, the rabbeted area is automatically formed in the assembled door. See "Build a Better Door" on page 143 for this method.

Supplies
Rockler • rockler.com or 800-279-4441
1 8-pack walnut classic Shaker pegs
#21956, $9.99
Woodcraft • woodcraft.com or 800-225-1153
1 pair non-mortise hinges, #27G12, $2.25
2 ½" x ⅛" rare-earth magnets, #150951, $8.99 (pkg of 10)
Prices correct at time of publication.

AMAZING HOLD. For small drawers, a lock joint has incredible hold. While the short grain is brittle before assembly, when locked together, the joint is plenty strong.

With the joinery on the rails and stiles complete, add glue to the joints, assemble the door in clamps and allow the glue to dry. (After your finish is applied, install a clear Plexiglas panel, holding it in place with ¼"-square strips pinned in position.)

Drawer Joinery

Because this drawer is meant to house small parts and accessories, the joinery does not require superhuman strength. I built it using a down-and-dirty method: a lock joint cut at the table saw (the key to accuracy is set-up).

Mill your drawer parts to thickness, width and length. Install a dado stack in your table saw for a ¼"-wide cut, and set the blade height to ¼". Position the fence ¼" away from the stack, then cut dados at the ends of the drawer sides.

Now rabbet the ends of the back. I use a step-off block to align the stack with the ends of the front and back; a sacrificial fence is another option. Raise the blade height to ½", then rabbet the ¾"-thick drawer front.

With the blade height still at ½", switch over to a tenon jig to cut the tongues that lock into the dados. Position the jig and stack to cut dados leaving a ¼" of material at the inside face, as shown below.

When the cuts are complete and the parts fit properly, rabbet the bottom edge of the drawer front for the ¼"-thick drawer bottom. The bottom is pinned in place, but left overwide — you'll trim it to act as a drawer stop against the case back.

Drawer-front Design

A new approach for me was to texture the drawer front to add some visual interest with a series of grooves. I cut them with a ½" round-nose bit (also known as a core-box bit) at my router table, creating a series of small arcs in the front.

The secret (if there is one) is to start your layout, and the cuts, at the center of the drawer front and work toward the edges. Take the time to align the first cut down the centerline (it needs to be very close, but there is a bit of course correction possible from a second pass). After the first pass, reverse the front and make a second pass. This may widen your groove, but it will not be noticeable, and it guarantees you're centered. (As always, test pieces make setup easier.)

Slide your fence closer to the bit for the second and third grooves, making sure there is no flat between them. Repeat these steps for the fourth and fifth cuts (an odd number of grooves makes the layout much easier). With the drawer front textured, sand the grooves (a sandpaper-wrapped dowel works well), then glue up the drawer.

As the glue dried, I designed a few small pieces to use as pulls for the drawers and door. I began with ⁷⁄₁₆"-wide stock, then laid

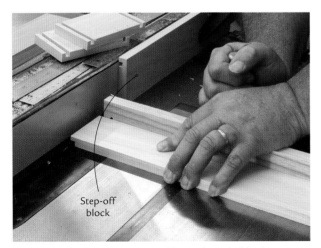

Step-off block

DADO STACK. Here, I'm cutting a rabbet on the end of the drawer back. Note the step-off block to align the workpiece with the blade.

FLUSH TO THE LIP. The last cut using the dado stack is to create the slot for the ends of the drawer sides. Position the cut at the top of the rabbet.

LAYOUT IS KEY. The first groove for the drawer-front texture should be perfectly centered in the face. (Or you can get darn close and make a second pass with the stock reversed.)

SUBSEQUENT GROOVES. Adjust the fence to make the next-in-line cuts in the texture pattern – working with grooves in odd numbers makes the layout work easier.

out a simple undulating pattern. I made the cuts at the band saw, smoothed the pieces at a spindle sander and eased the edges using sandpaper.

The drawer pulls are set into dados cut in the drawer front. Determine the location for the pulls (I used them to equally divide the two sections of the cabinet), then make marks along the edge of the drawer front to show the start and stop points of the dados.

Set your table saw blade to cut just below the deepest point of your decorative drawer grooves and align the blade with your

layout marks. Using the miter gauge, nibble away at the cuts until you've achieved the thickness of your pulls – check this with each pass when you get close to the second layout line. Repeat the steps for the second pull, then glue the pulls in place.

Wrap up work on the drawer by pinning the drawer bottom to the completed drawer box.

Fit & Finish

Fit the door to its opening, making any needed adjustments to its width and height. I used simple no-mortise hinges and a shop-made catch with two rare-earth magnets – one on the triangular catch, one buried in the door (don't glue the magnets in place before checking their polarity). The door pull is simply glued in place.

Lay out then drill holes in the router-bit shelves to accept the shanks of your router bits. Before installing the shelves in the cabinet, plane or cut the rear edges at a 15° angle to match the slope of the shelves, then slip them into their dados. The cabinet back holds the angled shelves in place.

The back is plywood. Install it with screws after completing the finish.

Here, too, I, decided to switch things up a bit from my usual approach. Instead of shellac, I used a water-based topcoat – Enduro-Var from General Finishes. And to try it two ways, I brushed on the first coat, but sprayed the second after a thorough sanding with #320-grit. (I wasn't surprised to find that I preferred the sprayed coat.)

My first thought as I finished the cabinet was that, had I not angled the router-bit shelves, this piece could have found its way into my house. But with the bit shelves in place, I've built a nice shop cabinet from something other than plywood. Plus, I played with a couple of new techniques along the way. And I have a great cabinet to help get a handle on my router bits and accessories.

RATHER CATCHY. A simple catch with a rare-earth magnet epoxied at the center is glued and pinned inside the door; another magnet is installed in the door.

Build a Better Door

As we gain experience in woodworking, we find or learn new techniques that make our work better. A great technique to up your door-building game is to produce doors, which, with a few extra steps, have rabbets already in place for glass or flat panels. No more rabbeting after assembly.

Here's how it's done: Mill the rails and stiles to length, width and thickness, then lay out and mark the mortises in your stiles; I chose ¼" shoulders for my tenons. Center the ¼"-wide x 1¼"-deep mortises in the stiles as you cut or chop the four mortises.

Now rabbet the inside edge of all four door parts. Cut ⅜"-wide rabbets as deep as the front wall of your mortises (½"). I prefer the table saw for this task, but there are other methods.

How the tenons are cut on the rails is where the huge difference in technique comes to light. Set the blade height to ¼" and set your fence to cut a 1¼" tenon. Don't forget to account for the blade kerf. With the rail's front face against the tabletop, make a pass cutting the rail.

Next, leave the blade height alone, but slide the fence to cut a ⅞" tenon (1¼"-⅜" rabbet). Make a pass cutting the rear face of your rails at all four locations. Before moving on, rotate the rail so the outside edge is facing the tabletop and make another cut. (There is no cut needed for the inside edge – it was removed by rabbeting.)

The difference in the procedure when making the cheek cuts is that you have two different blade heights with which to work: ⅞" for the back face and 1¼" for the front. Plus, you'll need to remove the shoulder waste using a band saw or handsaw.

As you slip the joint together, the extended shoulder at the back and outside edge of the rails fills the rabbeted area just as the front face snuggles tight to the stile. The rabbet for the glass or flat panel is done – and with no unsightly end-grain in sight.

1

After completing the mortises, rabbet the door parts flush with the front wall of the mortises.

2

Set the fence to cut a 1¼" tenon with the blade set to just pierce into the rabbet.

3

Readjust the fence for a ⅞" tenon on the rail's back face.

4

Cut the cheeks using two different height adjustments – one for the front face and a second for the back.

5

As the joinery slips together, the longer back tenons fills the rabbeted area just as the front tenon settles against the rail's edge.

ON THE SET. Roy Underhill's nail cabinet is a converted crate. The cabinet has seen a lot of use and has held up pretty well.

Chapter Twenty-Two

Roy Underhill's Nail Cabinet

by Christopher Schwarz

One of the enduring features of Roy Underhill's "The Woodwright's Shop" PBS television show is the familiar and rambling backdrop of former projects, parts, tools and wood that frames most episodes. My favorite item in his shop is his nail cabinet – a pine wall-hung cabinet tucked in the far back corner.

On the inside of the door of the cabinet, Roy has hung a print of a lovely lady holding a bock beer alongside an admiring goat. And while that's fun for the television cameras, I'm more attracted to the 21 drawers on the right side of the cabinet. These drawers are more useful to the married woodworker.

Nail cabinets show up frequently in traditional workshops of many trades, and they are illustrated and discussed in books about traditional shops. These cabinets stored the screws, nails and bolts that a workshop might need. And because these fasteners were valuable, many of the cabinets would have a lock.

The last time I visited Roy, I asked permission to measure and reproduce his nail cabinet, which he purchased during a yard sale in Washington, DC. As I measured the piece, I was bemused by its unusual construction – it was a finger-jointed carcase covered in nailed-on battens.

Then Roy showed me the reason for the odd construction: The cabinet was built from an old crate for Ohio Blue Tip Matches made by the Ohio Match Co. of Wadsworth, Ohio (1895-1987). For me, this made the project even more fun: I had to first build a crate and then turn it into a wall cabinet.

As a result, some of the construction techniques might seem a bit odd. If you don't like them, feel free to change them. My goal was to make a respectable reproduction of this charming cabinet because I've always liked the one on Roy's show.

Construction Overview

The original is made entirely of pine – probably Eastern white pine – though any dry softwood will do. The carcase of the original crate is joined at the corners with finger joints (though I opted for dovetails on my version). The back of the carcase is nailed-on ⅜"-thick boards that are shiplapped.

The assembled carcase is covered with narrow 1x battens to make the "crate" easy to grab and lift. These battens conceal the joinery on the corners of the carcase.

Once you have your "crate" built, you can turn it into a cabinet. The interior is divided into 21 spaces using thin pieces of pine that are joined with an egg-crate joint. The drawers are simply glued and nailed together; the only thing difficult about the drawers is that you have to build 21 of them.

Finally, the entire cabinet is fronted by a door with mitered corners. The panel of the original door was simply nailed to the inside of the mitered door frame. The panel had cracked over time, so I chose to make my panel float in grooves plowed into the rails and stiles.

The whole thing is finished with shellac and hung on the wall with a French cleat.

The Walls of the Crate

As mentioned above, the walls of the original crate were joined at the corners by narrow finger joints (you can see the joints from the inside where they have separated a bit). I don't have the jigs or desire to make narrow finger joints here, and cutting this machine joint by hand is just silly.

So I joined the case sides, top and bottom using through-dovetails. The joinery is all covered by battens in the end, so the end result looks the same as the original. For strength, I put the tails on the case sides; the pins are on the top and bottom bits.

Glue up the carcase, paying close attention to keeping the corners square at both the front and rear of the case. I use hide glue for joints like this because it's reversible.

If you can't get the case perfectly square at glue-up, you have one more chance to pull it square with the backboards. The backboards

GANG-CUT TAILS. Whenever possible, I gang-cut my tail boards, which saves time and (in my opinion) makes it easier to keep the saw 90° to the face of the board. A shallow rabbet on each tail board makes it easy to keep things square during transfer.

AS SQUARE AS POSSIBLE. Take extra pains to get the carcase square at glue-up. It will save you frustration later when you fit the door and the 21 drawers.

HIDE THE GAP. The shiplapped joints on the long edges of the back-boards hide any gap that would open up when the boards shrink in the dry season.

NAILS, NO GLUE. Nails will bend, allowing the back to expand and contract without splitting the backboards. Be sure to use nails with a pronounced head to hold the backboards in place.

are ⅜"-thick boards of pine that are shiplapped on their long edges and nailed to the back of the case.

I used 3d cut fine finish standard nails to affix the back, though 4d will do.

If your case is out of square, pull the case square with a clamp diagonally across two corners, then nail the backboards in place. This usually helps if the case isn't too racked.

The Interior Dividers

The interior drawer dividers of the original nail cabinet were obviously built up using miscellaneous scraps that were nailed and glued on to get the job done. Some parts were rough-sawn; some were different species.

Instead of replicating every odd scrap in the cabinet, I simplified the construction while still maintaining its look and function. On the original, the horizontal and vertical dividers are joined with egg-crate joints, and so I used that same joint for my dividers.

The dividers are all ⅜" thick and 6" wide. Every divider has ⅜"-wide slots cut into it. The slots on the horizontal dividers are

MORE GANG-CUTTING. Lay out the slots on one board, clamp all the dividers together and make the cut in one go. Here on the table saw, I'm using the saw's miter gauge and a high fence to push the dividers through the blade.

FRICTION & PINS. You should have to knock the joints together with a mallet. Then pin all the intersections with 1"-long headless brads. You'll have to nail them in diagonally to secure them.

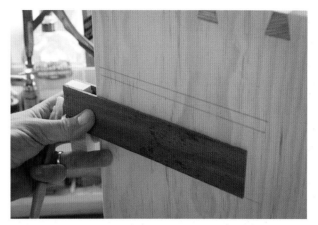

NAILING JIG. This scrap-wood jig helps you locate exactly where the horizontal dividers are located. It is made using two thin pieces of scrap that are nailed to a scrap of ½"-thick pine. Slip the jig onto the carcase and press one of the thin slips against the dividers inside the case. Trace its location on the exterior. Repeat.

AFFIX THE DIVIDERS. With the lines drawn on the carcase sides, drive in the cut headless brads and set them ¹⁄₁₆" below the surface.

Supplies

Lee Valley Tools • leevalley.com or 800-871-8158

1 knob, 17mm x 15mm, #01A05.17, $2.40

1 pair fixed-pin butt hinges, #00D03.02, $20.20/pair

7 flat knobs, 1¼" x 1", #02W30.22, $3.40 each

14 shell pulls, 3⅛", #02W30.26, $5.00 each

Prices correct at time of publication.

2⅞" long. The slots on the vertical dividers are 3" long. When the dividers are knocked together, they will be offset by ⅛" at the front, just like the original.

Lay out the locations of all the slots using the drawings as a guide. I used dividers to step off the drawer sizes, and I used an actual piece of the drawer divider to lay out the width of the slots. Note that the three bottom drawers are taller than the others.

I cut the slots on a table saw, though they are easy to cut by hand or on a band saw. After cutting the slots, knock the dividers together and pin the joints by toenailing them with headless brads.

With the dividers together, knock the assembly into the carcase. The front edge of the horizontal dividers should be located 1½" from the front edge of the carcase. That spacing allows room for the bin pulls and knobs on the drawers.

The next step is to nail the horizontal dividers to the carcase. This is done easily with a simple jig that makes it (almost) impossible to miss with your nails. (See the photo above for details on the jig.)

Use 4d headless brads to secure the horizontal dividers to the carcase. There's no need to nail the vertical dividers to the carcase; gravity and friction are sufficient.

Making It a Crate

The fun part of this project is taking this nice carcase and turning it into a packing crate. You do this by nailing on 1x battens so they look a bit like rails and stiles. There is no other joinery between the battens — just glue and nails.

Cut the battens to the sizes shown in the cutlist. The easy way to install these is to first attach them to the carcase sides, trim the pieces flush to the top and bottom of the case then finish up the work on the top and bottom.

The important thing to remember is that the battens should extend out ½" (or a tad more) from the front lip of the carcase. This ½" lip creates the opening for the door. Before you attach the battens, make sure their position works with the hinges you have purchased for the door. If the hinge leaf is wider than ½" you have

INACCURATE. The 45° setting on my iron miter box is off by about half a degree. But I don't mind. That's because I shoot my miters, which allows me to sneak up on the perfect length and angle.

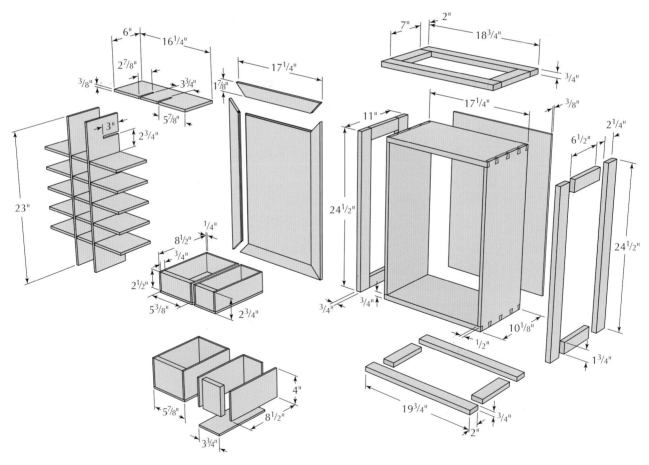

EXPLODED VIEW

to shift the battens forward a little on the case so the hinge can open and close.

All the battens are attached with brads and glue.

Mitered Door

With all the battens attached, you can determine the final sizes of your rails and stiles for the frame-and-panel door. The corners of this light-duty door are joined by miters that are glued and nailed, just like the original.

When I cut miters, I saw them first then trim them to a perfect length and a perfect 45° with a miter shooting board and a handplane.

Even if you love your miter saw, I encourage you to give this a try sometime. I've found no easier way to cut perfect miters. By shooting the miters with a handplane you can control the length of your rails and stiles in .001" increments. And you can hit dead-on 45° with ease.

Once the miters are cut, plow a $^{3}/_{16}$"-wide x $^{3}/_{16}$"-deep groove on the inside edge of the rails and stiles. The $^{3}/_{8}$"-thick panel fits into the groove thanks to a rabbet cut on all four edges of the panel. Be sure to size the panel so it has a little room for expansion and contraction in its width.

I don't own any fancy clamps for gluing mitered corners – most band clamps are fairly frustrating to use – so I glue up miters, corner by corner.

NAIL THE MITERS. A single nail through the stile and into the rail prevents things from sliding around as you clamp up this mitered joint. This was, by the way, how the original door was assembled.

Nail Cabinet

NO.	ITEM	DIMENSIONS (INCHES)			MATERIAL
		T	W	L	
2	Sides	½	10⅛	24½	Pine
2	Top/bottom	¾	10⅛	17¼	Pine
1	Back	⅜	17¼	24½	Pine
2	Door rails	½	1⅞	17¼	Pine
2	Door stiles	½	1⅞	24½	Pine
1	Door panel	⅜	13¾	21⅛	Pine
Top Frame					
2	Stiles	¾	2	18¾	Pine
2	Rails	¾	2	7	Pine
Side Frames					
4	Stiles	¾	2¼	24½	Pine
4	Rails	¾	1¾	6½	Pine
Bottom Frame					
1	Front stile	¾	2	19¾	Pine
1	Rear stile	¾	2	18¾	Pine
2	Rails	¾	2	7	Pine
Interior					
2	Vertical dividers	⅜	6	23	Pine
6	Horizontal dividers	⅜	6	16¼	Pine
12	Wide drawer fronts	¾	2½	5⅜	Pine
6	Narrow drawer fronts	¾	2½	3¼	Pine
2	Wide lower drawer fronts	¾	4	5⅜	Pine
1	Narrow lower drawer front	¾	4	3¼	Pine

First I spread a little glue on the two mating surfaces of the miter and let them dry for a minute. Then I add more glue to the joint. I press the two pieces together and drive a single nail through the stile and into the rail.

I repeat this process for each corner (don't forget to slide the panel into the frame before adding the last piece). Then I clamp up the joints using four ordinary bar clamps. The nails prevent the miters from sliding as you apply pressure at the corners.

21 Drawers

Because this is a cabinet for nails, it's appropriate that the drawers are nailed together. All the drawers are constructed in a simple manner: The front and back are captured by the sides. The bottom is then nailed on.

The drawers look a little odd – the end grain of the sides and bottom is visible on the drawer front. But they are acceptable for a piece of shop furniture – and the drawers in the original have survived many years of use.

Begin by fitting all the drawer parts for each opening. I try to do as much fitting as I can before assembly. This usually means the drawer will require little or no tweaking after assembly. First I fit each bottom to its opening. Then I fit the sides, front and bottom. Then I begin assembling the drawer.

BEGIN WITH THE BOTTOM. Get each bottom board to slide in and out of its opening before sizing the other drawer parts. If the bottom binds, the assembled drawer will bind.

TOO LONG? Dry-assemble the drawer to feel if the drawer front is too long.

GLUE THE BOTTOM. Because the parts are all softwood, which doesn't move much once it's dry, you can get away with both gluing and nailing this cross-grain joint.

SHOOT IT. If the drawer front is too long, shoot it to perfect length with a plane on a shooting board. Count your strokes. Then reduce the length of the drawer back by the same number of strokes, provided your original lengths were the same.

To do so, place the front and sides in position on the bottom. Feel if the drawer front needs to be reduced in length so the sides are flush to the bottom. If you need to trim the drawer front, trim the back by the same amount.

Glue and nail the sides to the front. Then glue and nail the back to the sides. Finally, glue and nail the bottom to the drawer. Fit each drawer to its opening, numbering the drawer and its opening as you go.

Hardware & Finish

As on the original, I used bin pulls for the larger drawers and knobs for the smaller drawers in the center. To ensure I got the bin pulls located correctly, I made a quick drilling jig that I clamped to each drawer front. The jig ensured I didn't make a layout error.

The knobs are located dead center in the fronts of the smaller drawers.

Were I to make changes to this cabinet, it would be with the hardware. While I like the bin pulls, it would be more helpful to have pulls like an old library card catalog; the card could tell you what type of fastener is inside the drawer.

To solve this problem, Roy simply wrote what is in each drawer on the bin pull. I think he did it with pencil – it's almost impossible to see on camera.

Another thought: Add 2" of depth to the cabinet and you can hang hammers, screwdrivers and other accoutrements of fastening and unfastening on the inside of the door.

Install the hinges and knob on the door. I used a magnetic catch to hold the door shut. Because I'm the only person who works in my shop, there's no need for a lock.

I finished the nail cabinet with two coats of garnet shellac, sanding between the coats. The cabinet hangs on my shop wall with a French cleat made from ½"-thick material.

And now comes the fun part: Emptying my tackle boxes of nails and screws and putting them into their new drawers, which are located conveniently above my workbench. Oh, and I guess I'll have to look for a picture of a lady and a goat.

INSURANCE. When I have to do something 14 times, you can bet I'm going to make a jig to ensure my mind doesn't wander and cause me to make a fatal error at this stage of the project. This simple jig locates the holes for the bin pulls in the correct place. For the taller drawers on the bottom, I set the jig ⅜" lower on the drawer front.

Saw & Plane Till

by Mike Siemsen

You've no doubt seen photos of the H.O. Studley tool cabinet – the Sistine Chapel of tool cabinets. And as far as I'm concerned, Studley got it right. Yes, his tool chest is a work of art and all that, but more importantly, it hangs on the wall.

With apologies to all you people who love floor chests, I prefer wall-hung tool storage if I don't have to travel and I have the wall space. I can see at a glance where my tools are and I find my access is easier.

This saw and plane till is open for easy access, but with a few modifications you could put doors on it to keep out humidity (or co-workers). It's also a simple matter to add a back.

First, Admit the Problem

I designed this till for my minion, Tod Twist (we don't have apprentices any more). Tod needed tool storage, and I needed fodder for an article.

Because you're reading a woodworking book, it's probably safe to assume that you have a saw or plane problem (or both).

This till holds 21 saws, the Stanley bench planes from No. 1 to No. 8 and a half-set of hollows and rounds. It has four drawers to store parts and sharpening equipment, saw sets, files and the like. I hang my saw vise from a nail in the side.

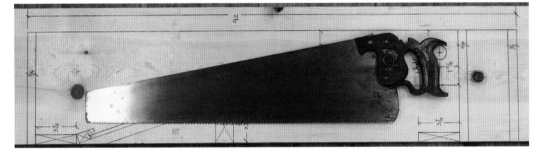

BESPOKE FIT. You can get an exact fit for your tools if you use them as the basis for your till's measurements.

ALL IN ONE. I used the same board to lay out dimensions for both the saws and planes – it's easy to tell them apart.

Saw & Plane Till

NO.	ITEM	DIMENSIONS (INCHES)			MATERIAL
		T	W	L	
2	Sides	¾	9⁵⁄₁₆	42	Pine
1	Divider	¾	9⁵⁄₁₆	41	Pine
1	Top	¾	9⁵⁄₁₆	50	Pine
1	Bottom	¾	9⁵⁄₁₆	50	Pine
2	Hanging cleats	¾	3½	50	Pine
1	Dowel	1¼ dia.		24⅞	Closet rod
1	Dowel	1¼ dia.		8	Closet rod
1	Saw separator*	1½	2½	23⅞	Pine
1	Rod support	¾	9⁵⁄₁₆	19⅝	Pine
2	Shelves	¾	9⁵⁄₁₆	24¼	Pine
1	Plane till panel	¾	23⅞	26⁹⁄₁₆	Pine
2	Plane till cleats**	¾	11½	23⅞	Pine
2	Plane till battens	¾	2¾	23⅞	Pine
8 or 9	Plane dividers	½	½	24	Pine
4	Drawer fronts	¾	3¼	11⅝	Pine
8	Drawer sides	½	3	8⁵⁄₁₆	Pine
4	Drawer backs	½	3	11⅝	Pine
4	Drawer bottoms	¼	8⁵⁄₁₆	11⅝	Pine

*1" notches, ⅛" wide, spaced 1" apart; **One cleat has a ½" x ½" rabbet.

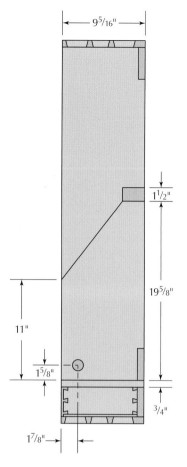

RIGHT PROFILE SECTION

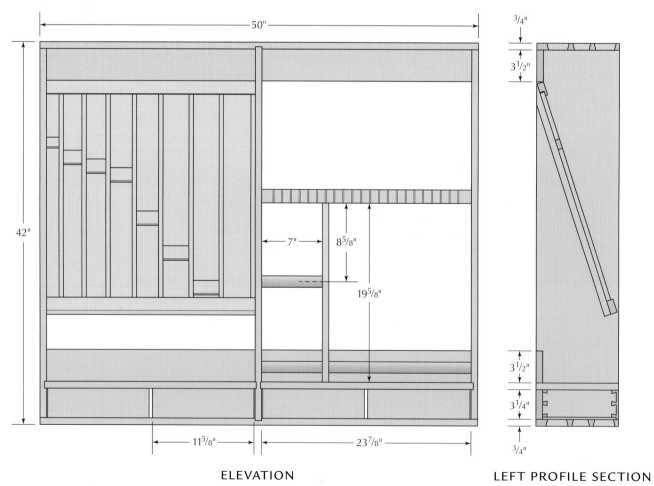

ELEVATION

LEFT PROFILE SECTION

ASSEMBLY REQUIRED. This exploded view of the till's components shows the blind holes for the support rods, the dados and the saw separator.

PLAYING THE ANGLES. One shelf is fastened with nails driven through the dado. For the other side, drive the nails in at an angle from the opposite side.

You can build just the saw till or the plane till, or combine them as we did. Feel free to make it wider or narrower as your needs dictate.

You can also omit the drawers. Be sure to leave "room for growing" like my mother did when she bought me clothes and shoes when I was a boy.

Made to Fit

We decided on lumberyard pine for our project. At first, Tod thought it was "curly pine" but then he realized it was just knife marks from the planer. We used 1x10 material, which made the case 9⁵⁄₁₆" deep after assembly.

I started by placing my longest saw on a board and marking the location of the dowel the totes would rest on, as well as where I thought the slotted separator that holds the sawplates should go.

From panel saw to half-rip to miter saw, I placed several saws on the drawing to ensure the placement worked for most saws. I did the same for the location of a higher dowel to hold shorter backsaws.

I used my longest plane to set the length of the plane till and work out the location of the rabbeted top cleat and the bottom cleat that the planes rest on.

I drew everything on the same board as the parts for the plane till are easy to tell from the parts for the saw till.

The outer case is joined with through-dovetails and dadoed for the shelves and divider.

Start Cutting

Once you are sure of your dimensions, cut your outside pieces to length.

Using a saw, chisel and router plane, Minion Tod and I cut ¼"-deep dados in the sides, top and bottom. Then we cut ⅛"-deep dados in either side of the center divider to hold the shelf pieces.

Cut the vertical rod support piece that will hold the short dowel rod and notch it for a hanging cleat. Make the same notches on the two ends and the center divider. When I hang a case like this, I just screw through the cleats and into the wall, but you could add a French cleat if you go for that sort of thing.

Now cut the dovetails, but be sure to remember the ¾" x 3½" notch for the hanging cleat when you lay out the dovetails at the top. The pins for the dovetails should be on the top and bottom boards for easier assembly.

Now bore the holes for the dowels that will hold the saw handles. Lay out and drill 1¼"-diameter blind holes ½" deep in the divider, case side and rod support piece for the long dowel. Then, drill a through-hole in the rod support for the long dowel.

Cut the long dowel to length (it should be 1" longer than the opening.) Cut the two hanging cleats to length (they should be the width of the case).

Sand the inside of the case to clean it up a bit, and you are ready to assemble. And go wash your hands — you don't want to dirty up your sanded parts.

Get It Together

Begin assembly by inserting one of the shelves into the dado in the center divider and drive a 6d nail through the opposite side of the dado. Insert the other shelf and fasten it with a 6d finishing nail driven from the bottom face of the first shelf. Angle the nails and set them with a nail set.

Center and attach the bottom cleat to the shelves with 8d nails driven from the bottom face of the shelf into the cleat. Then drive a 2" screw into the divider from the back of the cleat.

Center and nail the top cleat to the back edge of the top with 8d nails. Make sure you nail through the upper face of the top piece, or your dovetail pins and dado will be in the wrong orientation.

Insert the center divider into the dado in the top and screw the top to the divider with 1⅝" screws. Using 2" screws, attach the cleat to the divider. Insert the center divider into the dado in the bottom board and attach it with 1⅝" screws.

Slide the long rod through the rod support and insert the dowel into the lower blind hole in the center divider.

Apply glue to your dovetails and fit the ends to the top and bottom, making sure the rod goes into its blind hole and the shelf into its dado.

Screw the side to the shelf with 1⅝" screws. Drive 2" screws through the hanging cleats into the sides. Square up the case and let the glue dry.

Saw Separator

While the glue is drying, make the saw separator from a tight-grained 2x4. It should be the same length as the width of the opening it fits into.

Because saw handles are typically ⅞" thick, make the notches 1" on center. The notches are ⅛" wide and 1" deep. I used a powered miter saw for this because the blade cuts a ⅛"-wide kerf and has a depth stop.

Slide the rod support over to the divider and mark it at the top to locate the position of the saw separator; slide it over to the side and do the same.

Place the separator where you want it, leaving the number of slots you think you will need on either side of the rod support. Attach the separator with a 2" screw through the divider and the case side.

Measure and cut your short rod to 1" longer than the opening (because the blind holes are ½" deep). We used 8", giving us a 7" opening for Tod's backsaws.

HOLDING POWER. The cleats at the top and bottom run the full width of the case, fitting into notches on each side piece.

The rod support will center on a saw slot. To attach it, screw up through the shelf into the rod support and through the hanging cleat with a 2" screw and down through the separator with a 3" screw. If you decide to change the location of the rod support later, you can take out the screws and move it to where you want. You'll need to make another short rod or cut off the short rod you have, depending on which way you move the rod support.

Take a step back and admire your work! Enjoy a cool beverage and look around your shop, put some things away and tidy up a bit; savor your life.

Enough of that, get back to work!

Nice Drawers

For your drawer fronts, pick a nice ¾"-thick board the length of your case and the height of the drawer opening.

Cut four equal-sized drawer fronts from this board, allowing about ¹⁄₁₆" between the fronts in each opening. (After planing the sides there will be a bit more play.)

Keep your drawers in order so the grain will match along the fronts when the drawers are installed.

The drawers are dovetailed at the corners with the bottoms nailed on.

The sides and back of the drawers are ½"-thick material and are ¼" narrower than the opening and your drawer fronts. The bottoms are ¼" thick, the same length as the drawer front and ¼" narrower than the total depth of the drawer.

The drawer backs are the same length as the front. Each drawer side is ¼" less than the drawer depth.

We gang-cut the tails in the sides and cut half-blind dovetails in the fronts and through-dovetails in the back.

MATCHED SET. Use a single board for your drawer fronts to keep the grain matching across your till.

ORGANIC FORM. Tod created leather pulls and stamps, complete with his mark, for this till – exercise your creativity and make your till your own.

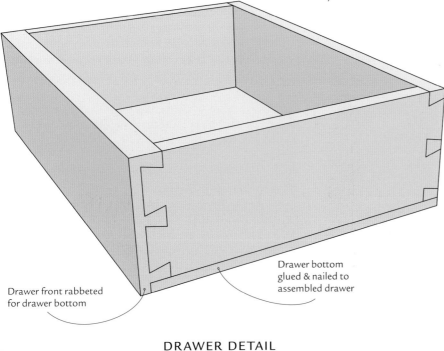

Drawer front rabbeted for drawer bottom

Drawer bottom glued & nailed to assembled drawer

DRAWER DETAIL

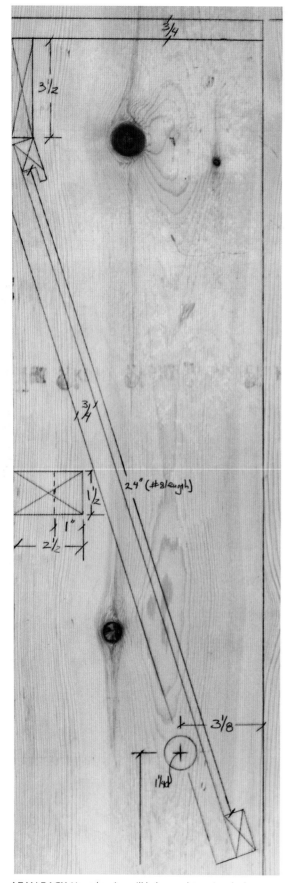

LEAN BACK. Your drawing will help you determine the best angle for your plane till for both clearance and good looks.

Cut a ½" by ¼"-wide rabbet in the bottom back edge of the drawer front to receive the ¼"-thick bottom. Glue and nail the bottoms on each drawer using ⅞" nails and setting the heads below the surface.

The grain in the bottom runs the same direction as the grain in the drawer front. Be sure to glue the front lip of the drawer to the bottom so it doesn't break off.

After the glue dries, plane the sides to clean them up and fit them to the case. While you're at it, plane to clean up the dovetails on the case.

The Right Order

Be sure to number your drawers so they will go back in the proper order. I like to use Roman numerals at the top edge of the drawer front.

A single chisel strike is a I; a double strike II; and so on. Look at a clock dial if you get stuck. (By the way, there are II kinds of people in the world: those who can read Roman numerals and those who can't.)

The drawer stops and drawer guides are actually four nails. To make the drawer stops and guides, first drill pilot holes and drop an 8d headed nail that is snipped to about 1¼" long through the shelf next to the divider at the inside edge of the drawer at the front corner. Then make similar holes through the shelf next to the carcase sides.

Put the nails about ¾" from the front edge and about 9⁄16" in from the verticals, where they will act as stops and rude guides for the drawers. To remove a drawer, just pull out the nail.

Tod is a leather worker, so he made leather pulls for his drawers and stamped them with his maker's mark.

Plane Till

Construct the plane till so it is the width of your opening and the length of the longest plane it will hold, plus 2⁹⁄16".

Refer to your drawing to see how much of an angle to put on the top back edge to create more clearance for the till.

Our plane till is just under 24" wide after assembly, so we used three pine boards, ¾" thick x 8" wide. The boards could be splined or joined tongue-and-groove, but we just butted ours together without glue.

Attach the top notched cleat (1½" x ¾" with a ½" x ½" rabbet) in the corner of the front face with some glue and small nails. Orient it with the rabbet on the lower back of the cleat, giving the plane toes a convenient retention lip. Set your longest plane in place and attach the bottom front cleat in the same way, leaving about ¹⁄16" to ease moving the plane in and out.

Flip the panel over and attach the 2¾" x ¾" back batten to the panel with 1¼" screws. The upper batten should be low enough that it doesn't stick out past the back and contact the wall when installed. The bottom batten is nailed flush to the bottom edge.

Fit the plane till in place with its top against the top hanging cleat and the bottom just behind the cabinet's front face. Mark around the ends with a pencil so you can locate your screw holes, then remove the panel.

Drill through the divider and the end inside the lines so the screws will go into the boards of the till. Three 2" screws per side

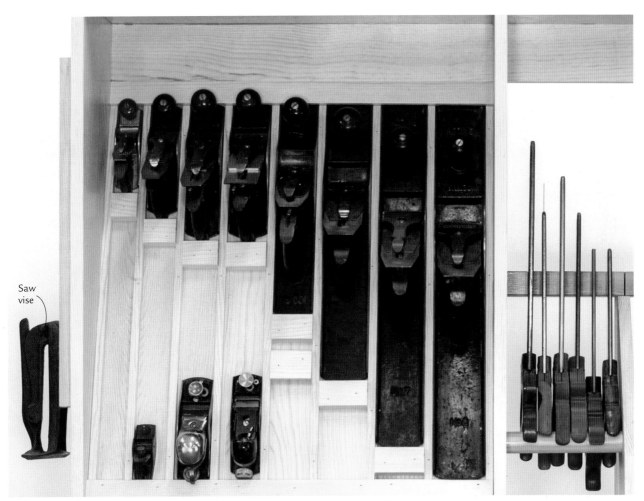

Saw
vise

RULER TRICK. A ruler and a few sticks are all you need to set the spacing between your planes.

should be plenty, with one screw 2" from each end and one in the center. You might need to move the screw locations around to avoid problems with saw till pieces on the other side of the divider.

Sticking Sticks

Make up a batch of square sticks to use as dividers for your planes – the number depends on the level of your plane-buying problem. The sticks need to fit under the rabbet in the top cleat, so they will be just under ½" square.

Using small nails, attach one stick to each outside corner of the till.

Set your longest plane in place, then place a ruler between the plane body and the next stick, then attach the stick.

Repeat the process for your next plane, using the plane and ruler to set the width. Next, cut a 1½" x ¾" block the width of the spacing (a plane plus ruler thickness) and nail that block in place below your plane, leaving just a bit of room to ease removing and replacing the plane.

If you have wooden planes, make a taller rabbeted block for the top and screw it to the till.

All of this is easier to do if you lay the till on its back.

Our opening just happened to be the right width to put in each plane from No. 1 through No. 8 so it looked nice for the photo.

Almost Done

Give everything a light sanding and a coat of your favorite finish. We used clear shellac.

While the finish is drying, figure out how high the bottom of the cabinet should be from the floor

Cut two pieces of 2x4 to that length, then locate your studs. Get a helper and set your cabinet on the 2x4s, have your helper hold the cabinet against the wall so it can't fall forward or move side to side. Drive 3" to 4" screws through the hanging cleat and into the studs.

After completing the till, we got the same question from several people. What goes in the space under the short backsaws? This is your own personal space, a place for your Chris Schwarz commemorative bobblehead from Woodworking in America 2004, first-aid supplies, your favorite emergency beer or just pile it full of marking gauges.

For me, it is a shrine for my St. Roy action figure complete with sharp tools and a wound that bleeds.

German Work Box

By David Thiel & Michael A. Rabkin

During a recent trip to Germany, our former publisher, Steve Shanesy, snapped some pictures of a utilitarian, but also clever, rolling tool cart used in one of the woodworking shops he visited.

The cart was designed to hold your tools so your bench or assembly platform remained tidy. It had doors and drawers on the lower section, plus wings that opened on top to reveal three tool wells that kept things orderly and prevented items from falling onto the floor. When not in use, the cart closed to a nice size and could even be locked.

The staff agreed that the idea was a good one, but we decided to put a Popular Woodworking spin on it. We divided and detailed the lower drawer space some more and added a tool till inside the center well with magnetic tool holders.

Plus we made sure the construction was simple. Mechanical fasteners do all the hard work. You could easily build this cart with a circular saw, a drill and a router, making it a great project for beginners or even a professional cabinetmaker in a production shop.

Affordable Space

While we didn't start out worrying about price, the finished bill is worth talking about. Using two sheets of good-quality ¾" shop-grade plywood and one sheet of ½" Baltic birch ply for the drawers, wood costs came in at about $125. The necessary hardware (there's a lot more than you might think imagine) comes in at less than $150 if you build it exactly as we have. So for $275, you're still getting a lot of storage for the price and the space is arranged to be exactly what you need, unlike a store-bought toolbox.

Cut the drawer dados in the case sides prior to assembly. We used a router to make the dados and a store-bought guide that clamps across the plywood to guide the router. You could just as easily clamp a straight board to the side to serve as a guide. Use two passes on each dado to achieve the full depth. This puts less strain on the router and the bit.

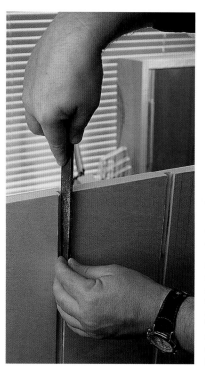

The veneer edge tape is easy to use and quickly adds a finished appearance to the cabinet. Even though we ended up painting the exterior, the paint still applied better to the veneer tape than on a bare plywood edge. You'll need to notch the tape with a file at the dado locations in the left case side.

The Basics

While this is a utilitarian work cart for the shop, we expended a little extra effort (veneer tape on the plywood edges and no exposed screw heads) to make it a more finished-looking project while maintaining the solid, simple construction details.

The cart joinery is a collection of butt joints. We used Miller Dowels, to assemble all the butt joints. This is a stepped wood dowel that replaces the screws and plugs the holes left by the drill bit at the same time.

The back is ¾" plywood (plywood offers great gluing strength on edge because of the long grain part of the plywood core). This size back offers excellent stability and the opportunity to square-up the case without worrying about wood expansion because of changes in humidity.

On the interior plywood drawers we used simple rabbet joints to add some extra strength. The bottoms of three of the drawers are screwed to the drawer boxes and stick out past the drawer sides to serve as effective drawer guides, emulating the metal drawers used on the right side of the case.

Begin With the Big Box

First cut the plywood panels to size according to the cutting list on page 164.

To allow the three smaller drawers to slide in and out of the case, you need to cut ½"-wide x ⅜"-deep dados in the left side of the case and in the left side of the center divider. Lay out the dado locations — according to the illustrations — then cut them using either a dado stack in your saw, repeated cuts with a circular saw, or with a straight bit, using two passes to achieve the full depth. There is ½" of space between each of the drawers and we worked from the bottom up, leaving a larger gap above the top drawer to allow clearance for the door catches.

Dowels & Glue

As mentioned, we used veneer tape to dress up the edges of the plywood. We had been using iron-on veneer tape for years, but recently discovered a self-adhesive veneer tape that is much simpler to use, takes the concern out of the glue melting evenly and sticks very well to the work.

After veneering all the exposed edges, sand the interior surfaces through #150-grit. Now you're ready to assemble the case.

Start by clamping the divider between the upper and middle shelves, holding the front edges flush. We used regular #8 x 1¼" screws here because they would be hidden inside the case. Drill and countersink ³⁄₁₆"-diameter clearance holes through the shelves and drill ³⁄₃₂"-diameter pilot holes in the divider. Add glue and screw the assembly together.

Next use either screws or Miller Dowels to attach the back to the center assembly. Check the spaces to ensure they are square, then add the bottom shelf to the back, holding the back flush to the bottom side of the shelf.

Clamp your center assembly between the two sides, drill the appropriate holes, add glue and assemble the rest of the case. It's a good idea to trim the dowels flush to the case side before flipping the case onto that face: It's more stable and there's less chance of messing something up.

Add the front piece to the front edges of the sides, holding it flush to the top edge. The front will overlap the top shelf, leaving ¼" of the shelf edge exposed. This allows room to attach the front to the shelf with brad nails. The exposed edge will act as a door stop once hinges are installed.

The wings go together like simple versions of the case. The side closest to the cabinet on each wing is ³⁄₁₆" narrower than the other. This creates a recess to house the hinge to mount the wings to the cabinet.

Screw the divider between the top and middle shelves by first drilling a pilot hole for the screws and countersinking the flathead screws to the shelf surfaces.

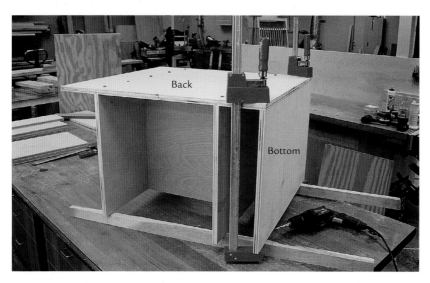

Attach the back to the center assembly using the Miller Dowels. Put glue on the back edges of the center pieces, then position the back and clamp it in place. After using the proprietary stepped drill bit to make the holes, add glue to the dowel and then tap it into place in the hole. Lastly, attach the bottom to the back with stepped dowels.

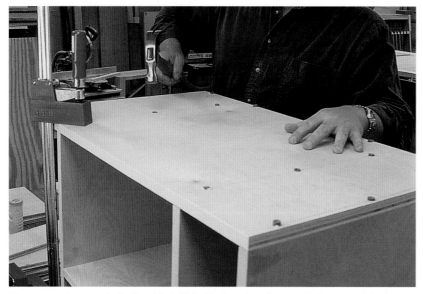

The next step is to attach the first side (which side doesn't really matter). Carry your location lines from the back around to the side and use them to lay out the dowel locations. Add glue, clamp, drill and dowel the joint.

Before attaching the second side, it makes sense to cut the dowels on the first side flush to the surface. I used a Japanese flush-cutting pull saw that has teeth with very little set to them, reducing the chance of scratching the cabinet side. By applying pressure on the blade to keep it flat to the cabinet surface, I further reduced the chance of scratches. Do a little sanding, then flip the cabinet over and attach the second side, then the front.

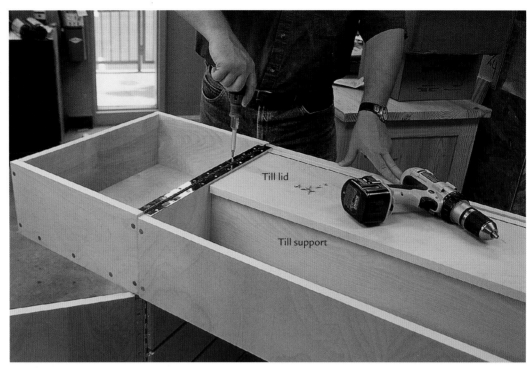

After attaching the till lid, the wings are ready. The wings are held flush to the front and are tight against the cabinet side. The recessed wing side is the attachment point for the piano hinge, allowing the lid to close flush against the top of the cabinet.

Till lid

Till support

German Work Box

NO.	LET.	ITEM	DIMENSIONS (INCHES)			MATERIAL
			T	W	L	
Case						
2	A	Sides	¾	19¼	32	Shop plywood
3	B	Shelves and bottom	¾	18½	28½	Shop plywood
1	C	Back	¾	28½	32	Shop plywood
1	D	Front	¾	67/8	30	Shop plywood
1	E	Divider	¾	18	18	Shop plywood
2	F	Doors	¾	14¹⁵⁄₁₆	25	Shop plywood
4	G	Wing front and back	¾	6¹⁵⁄₁₆	15	Shop plywood
2	H	Wing sides	¾	6¹⁵⁄₁₆	18½	Shop plywood
2	I	Wing sides	¾	6¾	18½	Shop plywood
2	J	Wing panels	¾	13½	18½	Shop plywood
1	K	Till support	¾	5½	28½	Shop plywood
1	L	Till lid spacer	¾	¾	28¼	Maple
1	M	Till lid	¾	10	28¼	Shop plywood
2	N	Drawer section sides	½	12	18	Shop plywood
Drawers						
2	O	Drawer front and back	½	4	15¾	Baltic birch
2	P	Drawer sides	½	4	17½	Baltic birch
2	Q	Drawer front and back	½	4½	15¾	Baltic birch
2	R	Drawer sides	½	4½	17½	Baltic birch
2	S	Drawer front and back	½	5	27½	Baltic birch
2	T	Drawer sides	½	5	17½	Baltic birch
2	U	Drawer front and back	½	5½	15¾	Baltic birch
2	V	Drawer sides	½	5½	17½	Baltic birch
3	W	Drawer bottoms	½	16¾	18	Baltic birch
1	X	Drawer bottom	½	17½	27	Baltic birch

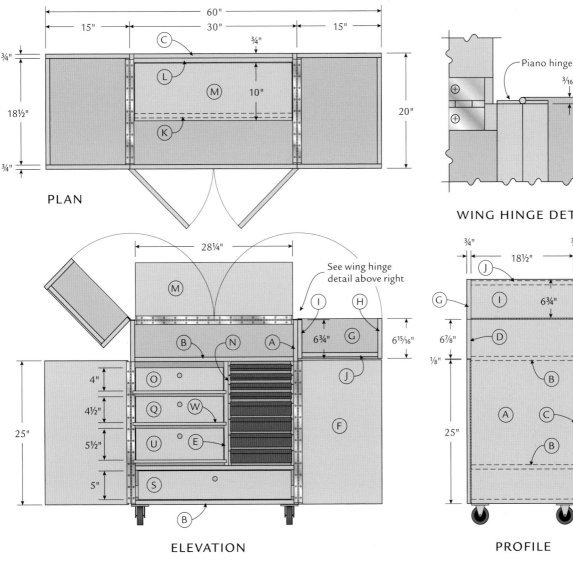

PLAN

WING HINGE DETAIL

Piano hinge

ELEVATION

See wing hinge detail above right

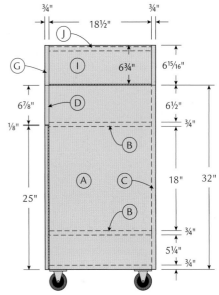

PROFILE

We recessed the captured panels ¼" in from the outside edges to avoid any alignment problems. Using the stepped dowels, attach the wing sides to the wing panels. Attach the fronts and backs to complete the assembly.

Storage Details

Start by adding the till lid to the back with a length of continuous (or piano) hinge. Because of the way the hinge needs to mount inside the cabinet (so the wings can close) we added a ¾" x ¾" maple strip to the back ⅛" down from the top edge. This allows the till lid to open to about 110°. Mount the lid to the strip with a length of piano hinge. Carefully check it for clearance between the two sides as it closes.

Next, attach the till support to the top shelf by screwing into the support through the shelf. The support is set back ½" from the front edge of the till lid to allow you to get your fingers under it to lift the lid. Add some glue and a couple of stepped dowels through the sides to hold everything in place.

Now you need to attach the two wings to the case with more piano hinge. Clamp the wings to the case in the open position

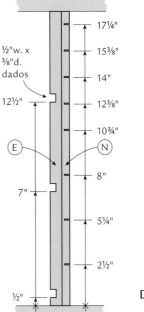

½"w. x ⅜"d. dados

DRAWER DADO LAYOUT

(flush to the front) while attaching the hinges to ensure even and well-supported wings.

Lastly, attach the doors to the case (use a piano hinge again). To get the doors to seat flush against the cabinet front, cut a shallow rabbet ($\frac{3}{16}$" deep, the thickness of the hinge) the width of the closed hinge on the back of the door on the hinge side. This cut can be done with your router or table saw.

When attaching the doors, pay careful attention to the height. Preferably they will be about $\frac{1}{8}$" below the wings when open to keep things from bumping.

You'll also notice that the left-hand door's hinge covers the dados for the drawers. Rather than place the hinge on the outside of the cabinet (making it too visible), we opted to simply file out the hinge to match the dado locations, as shown below.

Drawer Space

Ultimately you'll decide how the interior space in your cart is used. We've used drawers because our experience has shown that low shelving just collects junk at the back of the case that you can never see or reach easily.

We've used a selection of drawer types for this project, both shop-made and purchased. You can follow our lead or choose whatever style you prefer.

The lower shop-made drawer is simply a Baltic birch box drawer mounted on full-extension, 100-lb. drawer slides. This is a fine heavy-duty drawer joined at the corners with simple rabbet joints. We used a $\frac{1}{2}$" bottom fit into a rabbet in the sides. While we usually would have recommended a $\frac{1}{4}$" bottom, we had the $\frac{1}{2}$" material and didn't feel like by buying a whole sheet of $\frac{1}{4}$" for just one drawer.

The store-bought drawers are metal, lighter-duty drawers of 1" and 2" depths and have metal flanges that ride on dados cut into the sides of the case. With these, the front of the drawer overlaps the case sides to both hide the dados and serve as a drawer stop. As this would interfere with the door hinge, we added two drawer section sides made of $\frac{1}{2}$" Baltic birch and set them back 1" from the front of the case. This also made it possible to cut the dados in the section sides after the case was assembled.

The three drawers to the left use the best of both worlds, finishing off some of the wood at hand and avoiding the cost of more drawer slides by using the "lip and groove" concept of the metal drawers. On all the wood drawers, a simple 1" hole drilled in the front serves as an adequate drawer pull.

Finishing Touches

The last steps are adding a finish (we opted for two coats of dark green latex paint on the outside; the inside was left as-is) and then some sturdy $2\frac{1}{2}$" casters to the case and placing and organizing your tools. The photos will show you a couple of storage tricks and items you can purchase to help keep things neat and tidy.

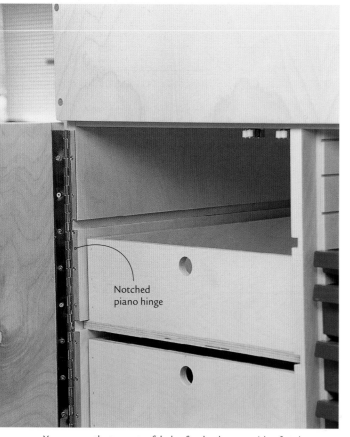

You can see the two sets of dados for the drawers with a few drawers removed. Also, notice the notched piano hinge to allow the drawers to slide in and out.

Notched piano hinge

Rabbet joint

Trimmed to fit

This shot of one of the drawers shows the rabbet joinery used. Also note that the bottom was trimmed slightly in width to allow the drawer to move more smoothly in the dados.

Pads line the bottoms of the wing and till sections to keep tools from rolling and to help trap dust. Dividers in the till section can be customized to fit the tools you need. The magnetic bars on the till lid provide secure storage for small ferrous tools. Small-parts storage is easily accomplished with a couple of plastic storage bins held in place in one of the metal drawers with some hook-and-loop fasteners.

$30 Lumber Rack

by Christopher Schwarz

In my family, we still remember the day my old lumber rack collapsed. I was upstairs with the kids when there was a sudden and horrible crash. The two cats ran in four directions; the baby started to wail. It was that loud.

When I went down the steps to the shop it looked like a giant box of toothpicks had spilled everywhere. It seems the metal brackets I had bolted to the walls had reached their limit. One of the brackets gave way and everything came tumbling down.

So when I went to rebuild, I wanted something stout, simple and cheap. I pored over books and magazines for ideas, borrowed a few and made some changes. Here's what I came up with:

Pipe & 2x4s

Essentially, the backbones of this rack are 2x4s bolted on edge to the double top plate and the bottom plate of my shop wall. The bottom edges of your 2x4s should rest on something solid. In most shops, that means running them to the floor. In my shop, the lower half of my wall is cinder block, so I set the 2x4s on those. To hold the lumber, I drilled ⅞"-diameter holes through the 2x4s at 4" intervals and at a 5° angle. Then I inserted 12" lengths of ½" galvanized pipe in the holes. The ½" pipe, available in the plumbing section, actually has an exterior diameter of just under ⅞", so it fits nicely.

Before you get started, there are a couple things to consider when building this rack for your shop. First, I used 12" lengths of pipe because I rarely have anything in my rack wider than 8". Wider lumber needs longer pipes. Plus, this rack is right over my jointer, so I didn't want the pipes to stick out any more than necessary.

Prep Your Lumber

I bought a single Southern yellow pine 2x8 that was 8' long for this project. By ripping it down the middle and crosscutting it into 4' lengths, I got four 4'-long 2x4s. If you don't have Southern yellow

pine in your area, try vertical-grade fir or any other tough construction timber.

I ran the parts over my jointer and through my thickness planer to get them straight and true. They finished out at 1⅜" thick and 3" wide.

Clearance Holes

The first thing to do is taper the ends of the boards and drill the clearance holes to bolt them to your wall. I used 4½"-long lag screws and 1⅜"-diameter washers. You want the holes in your boards to be clearance holes — that is, you want the threads on the lag bolt biting only into the wood in the wall.

Clamp all your pieces together when laying out the holes. This is faster and more accurate.

Because the table is at a 5° angle, it's easier to align your holes using the rim of the Forstner bit instead of the center spur.

Examine the diagrams and you'll see that the easiest way to accomplish this is to taper the ends as shown. I used a band saw to cut the taper and cleaned up the cut with a handplane.

The holes for the lag screws should be located so the screws enter into the top plate and bottom plate of your stud wall. The location of the hole in the diagram is for a stud wall with a double top plate. Your wall may be different.

Now drill a 1⅜"-diameter recess for the washer — it only needs to be deep enough to seat the washer. Then drill a ½"-diameter hole in the middle of the recess. Repeat this process on the other end of the board and on the other boards.

Even More Drill Press Work

Now, drill the holes for the galvanized pipe. Chuck a ⅞" Forstner bit in your drill press and set the table at a 5° angle. This slight angle will use gravity to keep your lumber in the rack.

Clamp all the pieces of wood together with the ends aligned and make a mark every 4" across all four boards.

Now drill the holes through the boards. Because the table is at 5°, it's difficult to get the center of the bit to hit your line. So don't. Instead, align your holes so the edge of the Forstner bit touches the line instead of the center. It's much easier.

Pipes & Installation

I bought galvanized pipe and cut it to length using a hack saw. Dress the ends using a grinder or file to remove the rough spots. Now get ready to install your rack.

Use a level to ensure your layout lines are plumb and parallel. Mark where the bolts will go and drill pilot holes for the lag screws. Fasten the lag screws to the wall using a ratchet.

I think you'll see quickly how nice it is to have a flexible rack like this. You can reserve a couple pipes for short scraps, and add more pipes or braces as your lumber pile expands.

$30 Lumber Rack

NO.	ITEM	DIMENSIONS (INCHES)			MATERIAL
		T	W	L	
4	Vertical braces	1⅜	3	48	Yellow pine
16	Pipes	½ID		12	Galvanized pipe
8	Lag screws			4½	
8	Washers	1⅜ dia.			

ID=interior diameter; the exterior diameter of this pipe is just under ⅞".

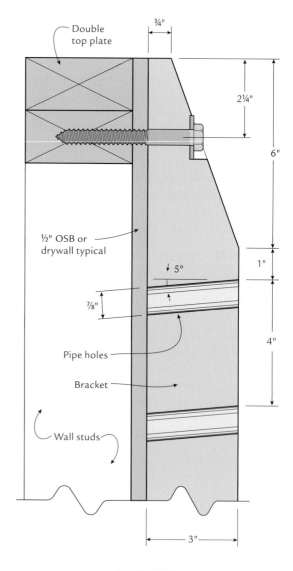

Double top plate

¾"

2¼"

6"

½" OSB or drywall typical

5°

⅞"

1"

Pipe holes

Bracket

4"

Wall studs

3"

SECTION

Index

Contributors

Graham Blackburn
Graham has been making furniture for more than 40 years. He is the author of numerous books on the craft – most recently "Jigs & Fixtures for the Hand Tool Woodworker" (Popular Woodworking).

Scott Gibson
Scott is a woodworker and writer who has edited for *Fine Homebuilding*, *Home Furniture* and *Fine Woodworking*.

Eric Hedberg
Eric is a designer and builder of specialty furniture. He lives and works in St. Paul, Minnesota.

Glen D. Huey
Glen is a former senior editor for *Popular Woodworking Magazine* and the author of several woodworking books.

Frank Klausz
Frank is a master cabinetmaker, author and owner of Frank's Cabinet Shop in Pluckermin, N.J.

Robert W. Lang
Robert is a former senior editor for *Popular Woodworking Magazine* and the author of several woodworking books.

Michael A. Rabkin
Michael is a former copy editor for *Popular Woodworking Magazine.*

Christopher Schwarz
Chris is a former editor of *Popular Woodworking Magazine* (now contributing editor) and is the editor at Lost Art Press.

Troy Sexton
Troy Sexton designs and builds custom furniture and is a private woodworking instructor in Sunbury, Ohio, for his company, Sexton Classic American Furniture.

Steve Shanesy
Steve is a former editor and publisher of *Popular Woodworking Magazine* and Popular Woodworking Books.

Mike Siemsen
Mike operates Mike Siemsen's School of Woodworking in Minnesota.

Jim Stuard
Jim is a former associate editor for *Popular Woodworking Magazine.*

David Thiel
David is a former senior editor for *Popular Woodworking Magazine* and now creates videos for the Popular Woodworking brand.

Don Williams
Don was a senior furniture conservator for almost three decades with the Smithsonian Institution. He is the project leader for the ongoing production of André Roubo in English; his work can be followed at donsbarn.com.

The Practical Workshop. Copyright © 2017 by Popular Woodworking Books. Printed and bound in China. All rights reserved. No part of this book may be reproduced in any form or by any electronic or mechanical means including information storage and retrieval systems without permission in writing from the publisher, except by a reviewer, who may quote brief passages in a review. Published by Popular Woodworking Books, an imprint of F+W Media, Inc., 10151 Carver Rd. Blue Ash, Ohio, 45242. First edition.

Distributed in Canada by Fraser Direct
100 Armstrong Avenue
Georgetown, Ontario L7G 5S4
Canada

Distributed in the U.K. and Europe by
F+W Media International, LTD
Pynes Hill Court
Pynes Hill
Rydon Lane
Exeter
EX2 5SP

Tel: +44 1392 797680

Visit our website at popularwoodworking.com or our consumer website at shopwoodworking.com for more woodworking information.

Other fine Popular Woodworking Books are available from your local bookstore or direct from the publisher.

ISBN-13: 978-1-4403-5122-8

21 20 19 18 17   5 4 3 2 1

Editor: *Scott Francis*
Designer: *Daniel T. Pessell*
Production Coordinator: *Debbie Thomas*

fw
a content + ecommerce company

Read This Important Safety Notice

To prevent accidents, keep safety in mind while you work. Use the safety guards installed on power equipment; they are for your protection.

When working on power equipment, keep fingers away from saw blades, wear safety goggles to prevent injuries from flying wood chips and sawdust, wear hearing protection and consider installing a dust vacuum to reduce the amount of airborne sawdust in your woodshop.

Don't wear loose clothing, such as neckties or shirts with loose sleeves, or jewelry, such as rings, necklaces or bracelets, when working on power equipment. Tie back long hair to prevent it from getting caught in your equipment.

People who are sensitive to certain chemicals should check the chemical content of any product before using it.

Due to the variability of local conditions, construction materials, skill levels, etc., neither the author nor Popular Woodworking Books assumes any responsibility for any accidents, injuries, damages or other losses incurred resulting from the material presented in this book.

The authors and editors who compiled this book have tried to make the contents as accurate and correct as possible. Plans, illustrations, photographs and text have been carefully checked. All instructions, plans and projects should be carefully read, studied and understood before beginning construction.

Prices listed for supplies and equipment were current at the time of publication and are subject to change.

Metric Conversion Chart

TO CONVERT	TO	MULTIPLY BY
Inches	Centimeters	2.54
Centimeters	Inches	0.4
Feet	Centimeters	30.5
Centimeters	Feet	0.03
Yards	Meters	0.9
Meters	Yards	1.1

Ideas • Instruction • Inspiration

Receive FREE downloadable bonus materials when you sign up
for our FREE newsletter at **popularwoodworking.com**.

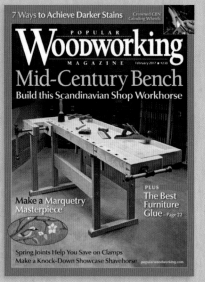

Find the latest issues of *Popular Woodworking Magazine* on newsstands, or visit **popularwoodworking.com**.

These and other great Popular Woodworking products are available at your local bookstore, woodworking store or online supplier. Visit our website at **shopwoodworking.com**.

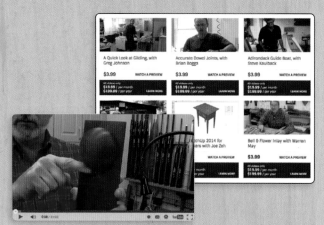

Popular Woodworking Videos

Subscribe and get immediate access to the web's best woodworking subscription site. You'll find more than 400 hours of woodworking video tutorials and full-length video workshops from world-class instructors on workshops, projects, SketchUp, tools, techniques and more!

videos.popularwoodworking.com

Visit our Website

Find helpful and inspiring articles, videos, blogs, projects and plans at **popularwoodworking.com**.

For behind the scenes information, become a fan at **Facebook.com/popularwoodworking**.

For more tips, clips and articles, follow us at **twitter.com/pweditors**.

For visual inspiration, follow us at **pinterest.com/popwoodworking**.

For free videos visit **youtube.com/popwoodworking**.

Follow us on Instagram **@popwoodworking**.